BARBARA HOSKING
EXCEEDING MY BRIEF

MEMOIRS OF A DISOBEDIENT CIVIL SERVANT

Biteback Publishing

This edition published in Great Britain in 2019 by
Biteback Publishing Ltd
Westminster Tower
3 Albert Embankment
London SE1 7SP
Copyright © Barbara Hosking 2017, 2019

ISBN 978-1-78590-462-2

10 9 8 7 6 5 4 3 2 1

A CIP catalogue record for this book is available from the British Library.

Set in Adobe Caslon Pro

Printed and bound in Great Britain by
CPI Group (UK) Ltd, Croydon CR0 4YY

For Margaret, who has kept me on course
for more than twenty years – so far.

CONTENTS

PREFACE

When their day's work underground was done and they made the long ascent to the surface, Cornish miners used the phrase 'coming up to grass'. I came up to grass when I was seventy-five years old and my years of work had finally finished. Or so I thought...

I write this memoir as I look back on an unplanned career which took me light years away from the sea and the Cornish cliffs and moors of my childhood. My ambition always was to write, and to have writers as my friends. I never imagined that cinema advertising, parliamentary press releases or speeches would flow from my pen. My ambition was to be a 'real' writer, like the authors I met when I invited them to speak at our school or interviewed in the Isles of Scilly, or whose manuscripts I typed up at Miss Wesley's secretarial college. Now, I have many authors among my friends, and I know first-hand how hard it is to face a blank page and write every day.

I had never expected to be professionally involved in politics, or to be a Cornish Liberal working for – indeed, becoming a supporter of – the Labour Party. I didn't foresee that I would be offered a marginal parliamentary seat, or come to admire and like many Conservatives, both within and beyond government. And I certainly never expected to receive an honour, yet I ended up with two, first an OBE and later a CBE. In ordinary social life, there is never an opportunity to wear honours, and I envy the French who wear little ribbons in their buttonholes to show that they have been awarded the Légion d'Honneur. I think this is why the French have such good eyesight – they are trying to see what rank the recipient holds!

I had always assumed that, like the rest of my family, I would die young. Yet there I was in the early autumn of 2016 planning my ninetieth birthday party in November. For my seventy-fifth birthday, I commissioned a piece of music from Judith Bingham. It was played by the Ambache Orchestra – of which I was a board member – the only orchestra at the time run by a woman, at a party at the Reform Club. Edward Heath came along and made a speech: 'I always did what Barbara told me – and see where it got me!'

I did not embark on this memoir with publication in

mind, but because I wanted to set down my experiences of a world that has changed beyond recognition over my lifetime; in particular the world of British politics and government of which I enjoyed a worm's-eye view. Perhaps, too, I was drawn to a nostalgic revisiting of my life, and to saluting the many extraordinary people who have populated both my working and my personal life. It is difficult to become a published writer today; the financial risks are high in an age of electronic reading, and I'm neither a celebrated cook nor a top footballer, or even famous for being famous. However, I have achieved my ambition: I have written a book and, one way or another, I will see it in print. It may not have quite the impact of the Atlantic breakers on Cornish cliffs, but I hope it will amuse my friends, and perhaps others who would like to ascend the greasy pole of the political world.

My story is, I believe, proof that life is a lottery. Health, success and love are all a matter of chance, and I grabbed the many unexpected chances which came my way. But, above all, I have been blessed with so many true friends, the sort of friends who not only enrich one's life with their company, but give support and withhold judgement.

My life is fuller than it has ever been. In retirement, I anticipated a life filled with friends, travel, and the arts, but a life lived essentially alone. Once again I was wrong. I had known Margaret from my membership of the 300

Group, the 1980s movement founded to encourage more women to become Members of Parliament, and we were also both on the Council of the Royal Society of Arts. We became friends, but the possibility of a closer relationship had never occurred to me. Not only had she been married, but she was twenty years younger than me.

Happily, I was wrong about that, too, and in the words of the old music hall ballad:

> When I thought that I was past love
> It was then I met my last love
> And I loved her as I'd never loved before.

I am, indeed, a fortunate woman.

PART I

STORMING IN

CHAPTER ONE

The Penlee lifeboat disaster occurred in 1981, a week before Christmas. Two vessels were lost with all hands. A Danish ship on her maiden voyage and a lifeboat with an eight-man crew from the village of Mousehole in the far west of Cornwall.

A rescue helicopter had been dispatched from Culdrose naval base, but the storm was so violent that it was impossible to help. The pilot said later that, despite the huge seas, the lifeboat actually managed to get alongside the ship, and, speaking of the lifeboat men, he added, 'I have never seen such heroism. It was truly heroic.' The lifeboat signalled that it had the captain's wife and children safely aboard. That was the last message.

I was working at the Independent Broadcasting Authority (IBA) at the time, where I was responsible for public relations, explaining the regulation of commercial television and radio to the media and public. I was born in Penzance, and knew very well how this tragedy would affect the nearby village of Mousehole. In Cornwall, lifeboats are an important fixture in people's lives. From the Lizard around Land's End to St Ives, local men are proud to volunteer and there is rarely a shortage of crews. I also knew the impact of these deaths on a small community whose members are all related. The news of the Penlee tragedy brought back vivid memories of many nights spent waiting with flasks of tea and whisky for the Sennen lifeboat to return, and I recalled watching the Isles of Scilly lifeboat going out into a storm.

I knew money would be needed and I wanted to help. First, I contacted the Mousehole Male Voice Choir. Would they give a concert in London to raise funds? They would. Next on the list was the head of public relations at Barclays Bank, who offered to lend me accommodation in West London, normally used for trainee bankers (Barclays incorporated the Cornish Bolitho Bank and so had strong links with Cornwall). I asked Thames Television if I could borrow their theatre. Yes, I could. With all this in place, I would organise a concert to raise money for the families left behind.

But I had completely forgotten one vital point: the media. This was a huge Christmas news story, and money immediately started rolling in. By Christmas Eve some two million pounds had been raised. My concert in the little Thames theatre would be a drop in the ocean. I then received a telephone call from Brenda Wootton, a great Cornish singer.

'Barbara,' she began, her voice sounding, like most Cornish voices, as if she were shouting into the teeth of an Atlantic gale. 'Could you take delivery of 1,000 pasties at Paddington Station for the concert?'

What?! We might possibly sell 100 Cornish pasties at the concert if we were lucky, but what would I do with the other 900? Very reluctantly, I decided to abandon the idea of a concert and leave the fundraising to more experienced hands. Next day, the fund totalled over three million pounds. Wonderful pictures of the headlands I used to walk over and the village I knew so well, where there are cannonballs from ships of the Spanish Armada in the churchyard, were shown on television. The storm had subsided and, as so often in Cornwall, Christmas Day was as mild as spring.

I felt very homesick and overcome by memories of childhood.

I was born to candlelight and to water. I had been told that there was a storm blowing the night I was born, with the sound of crashing waves. As darkness fell, all the lights went out. This was 4 November 1926, and the General Strike had reached the far west.

To complete this inauspicious arrival, my right arm was hanging in a strange way, but those Cornish nurses at the nursing home in the 1920s knew what to do with a sickly baby. As soon as the doctor had gone and my mother was asleep, they wrapped me up warmly and took me for an early morning walk along the promenade 'to get some good sea air into her little lungs'. If babies imprint like birds, then I was imprinted with a huge love of rough seas and a strong wind. But that could be Celtic. All Celts from Galicia to the Hebrides feel the same pull.

My mother returned with her baby daughter to the family dairy, where we lived over the shop. She was apologetic. My parents already had one daughter, my sister Peggy, and my father longed for a son. He had been a soldier – a very good soldier – during the Great War eight years before. He loved discipline, order and the company of men. Now, he had another girl, and one with a broken arm. Two years later, however, his wish was granted when my brother, Geoffrey, was born; and then, in 1930, my mother produced yet another daughter, whom they named Sheila. That was my family: my parents, William and Ada, two sisters and a brother.

For me, it was an unsatisfactory sequence because I lacked proper definition. I wasn't the eldest, or the youngest, or the only boy. Perhaps that is why I have never known my place. My right arm was a case of Erb's palsy, a very rare condition indeed, but shared with the German Kaiser. Historians read a great deal into its effect on his character; mine just made me fiercely independent.

Our dairy was in Causewayhead, roughly at right angles to Market Jew Street, the two main shopping streets in Penzance. They were separated by the Green Market where, after the cattle sales on market day, heavy-set farmers in their best breeches and jackets, gold watch chains straining across their stomachs, would sit smoking their strong cigarettes and watching the great world go by.

Our friends were not only other shopkeepers, but also included doctors, architects, hotel owners. My mother sang with them in the Operatic Society and my father met them at Masonic evenings. There were also artists in Newlyn, Lamorna and St Ives whom we knew, although it was difficult to place them. They spoke with upper-class accents but dressed scruffily, and were often drunk.

Our house in Causewayhead had no electricity. We had gas mantles in every room, which were very fragile and had to be carefully lit. If, by accident, a match knocked into the mantle, it disintegrated, and they were expensive to replace. Gas heated all the water for the bathroom and the kitchen. I must have been seven years old before I was allowed to stand on a chair, turn on the gas, strike a match, hold my breath and swiftly light the gas.

My mother loved the gas company. They held lectures

and cookery demonstrations that were hugely popular with the ladies of Penzance, the wives of professional men. They not only learnt new ways of cooking, but also enjoyed meeting a wider range of local people. The demonstrators, mostly from among the few women graduates of the time, later developed new careers as journalists or consumer advisers. It was here, as a demonstrator for the gas company, that Marguerite Patten began her career, before writing her very successful cookery books.

The gas cooker was also a convenient way out for those women who could no longer bear their often brutal lives. The sterling qualities of early twentieth-century man in isolated rural parts of the country had a real downside in battered wives and beaten children.

As long as we obeyed our father, family life above the dairy was happy for all of us, including our mother. Daddy was not really happy with a wife who loved the arts. The women in his childhood had worked ALL the time, milking, cooking, cleaning, and he often showed impatience with Mummy's failure to be house-proud. If he noticed dust on the sideboard or a leaf on the carpet, he would tut loudly.

> I will not marry thee
> A farmer's wife to be
> To do thy drudgery.

Life on Cornish farms was hard and there was no escape. Cows had to be milked every day, including Christmas, and there were always young children demanding attention in the kitchen, the warm heart of the farmhouse.

Boisterous laughter made Daddy uneasy. 'All this laughter will lead to tears,' he would say, a self-fulfilling prophecy as he cuffed one of us about the ears. He had another saying, which was most often delivered to me: 'There is a right way and a wrong way of doing everything. Why do you always choose the wrong way?' Mummy often began sentences with 'Shush! Shush! Your father is writing a cheque … Shush! Your father is listening to the six o'clock news…'

On days when we were well behaved, Daddy would take one of us, usually me, with him when he went to collect the milk. The others weren't too keen on rising before six, but I loved it. We would drive off in the big van and go from farm to farm around St Just, Cape Cornwall and Zennor, the sky turning blue and the sea and cliffs appearing as we went. We passed grey, dilapidated farm buildings clinging on to the steep hillsides, surrounded by 'hedges' of granite rock gouged out of the moors, laced with blackthorn, fuchsia and tamarisk, and golden with gorse.

There was much joking and gossip with the farmers, and sometimes a bun with clotted cream for me while the men loaded heavy churns of milk into the van. Daddy would tell me stories about the farms and their families and how we were related to them, and about the little granite churches. He showed me the medieval wooden carving of a mermaid in the church near the squint, and told me the story of the mermaid who fell in love with a choirboy and swam up the river at Zennor to take him back to sea.

He also told me about life in the army in India, about the dangers of the Khyber Pass, about how difficult it was to wrap puttees around one's calves in wet weather, about how good the Indian soldiers were and how he trusted them. And always about 'our Empire on which the sun never sets'. His dark eyes shone. 'I will make chapattis to-night,' he would promise, and he did.

My mother was keen to preserve Cornish traditions. 'You are entirely Cornish,' she told us. 'Your grandparents, great-grandparents, all the way back.' While I was still a baby, she took me to the Mên-an-Tol, a pair of prehistoric granite pillars, where I was pushed through the hole in the round, central stone. She performed the same ritual with my siblings. When I was older I asked her why. 'A bit of superstition, I suppose,' she replied. 'It does no harm to remember the old traditions.' Both my parents were superstitious. Crossed knives, shoes on the table, fishing on Sunday and many more bringers of bad luck had to be avoided.

On 1 May, all four of us children would be hauled out of

bed in the dark, given a quick breakfast and sent off to the woods with our May horns. These strange objects, which I have never seen outside Cornwall, were like megaphones. About three feet long with a mouthpiece, they were made of tin, and when you blew into them the noise was very loud indeed.

Our May Day task was to gather branches of leaves in the woods and wake the town up with our May horns as we came back. We were not the only children parading our green leaves, and the noise was deafening.

My parents' marriage was not happy. They had married for the wrong reasons. My mother had been unhappy at home in Newquay after her father had gone out to post a letter and dropped down dead when he was only thirty-four. He was an ex-miner who had gone out to Alaska in the Gold Rush of 1879 and had a little gold nugget on his watch chain. A year after his death, her mother married again, a widower with a son the same age as my mother. She favoured the boy over her own daughter, so when William Hosking came along, Ada saw him as a wonderful escape. And no wonder.

My father was good-looking, confident, a successful soldier back from the war. He had been the regimental sergeant major of the Duke of Cornwall's Light Infantry. His family were small farmers with a bit of land above St Ives which they had farmed for ever. He was the brightest of the children. When he met Ada, an educated young woman with a certificate for Voice from the Royal Academy of Music, a pretty face and a lovely nature, William saw her as a possible bride. And she was the only child of a mother, my grandmother, who was financially well off. It would be a good match. But my grandmother, who was a tough, practical woman, worried about her dreamy daughter's suitability as a wife for William. 'Always had her head in a book, or playing the piano,' she told me many years later, but at the time she kept her misgivings to herself.

The first few years in Penzance were probably the happiest time of Mummy's life. They lived over their brand new dairy, a wedding present from her mother. She had a young woman to help with the house full time, and a grumbling old woman for the rough work such as turning the mangle for the laundry on Monday mornings. Now that his mother-in-law had set him up in business, Daddy hired two men and bought a van for work and a car for us, one of the first cars in Penzance. When my elder sister Peggy was born, a second young girl was taken on as a nanny to help with her, and on her birth certificate my father was described as 'Master Dairyman'.

Our parents' social life was busy. They joined the local Operatic Society, where my mother was always given a good contralto role, while occasionally my father's sweet baritone was welcomed into the men's chorus. When I was old enough, I sometimes played the piano while my mother rehearsed; which is why I can still sing almost the whole of 'Samson and Delilah' in French!

There was a tiny cloud over the birth of my sister Peggy. The doctor, who was very popular in the town, made a forceps delivery, which involved clamping the baby's head on both sides of its forehead and pulling. The baby emerged unscathed, except for small scars like new moons by each eye, and a badly bruised right arm. Two years later, when she became pregnant again, my mother wanted to go to another doctor, but this was impossible because – so she explained to me later – we owed our doctor money. Perhaps that was why I was born with a broken right arm. Geoffrey and Sheila had a different doctor and they were fine.

When I was old enough, I started wearing an iron splint. It wrapped around my body and kept my arm above my head all day. That is how I acquired my nickname, Bobbie, because my father said I looked like a policeman directing traffic. As I grew, I was encased in a bigger splint: this was the medical solution to my problem in 1929. When I started going to school, I abandoned the splint in the evenings, and while this immobilisation slightly limited the length of my arm, I was still able to use it pretty well. It was then that Mummy had decided piano lessons would help.

Thursdays in Penzance were special. It was market day,

which was when all the farmers from around West Penwith came to town to sell their cows. By late morning, after the sales, they gathered in the Green Market. "'Ere, me 'andsome. 'Ow are 'ee?' they called, as they recognised an urban cousin, or 'Fine great girl she is!' as they compared notes on the local women and laughed coarsely.

"'Ow's it going then, William Henry?' they asked Daddy, as he joined them for a beer and pasty and discussed the price they had made for their cows. "'Tis less every month,' they complained, but my father envied them their hard life and loved their banter. He returned home late on market days, his face flushed and his eyes shining.

For a while he had been a man among men.

CHAPTER TWO

As the country entered the 1930s, the economic recession grew, unemployment increased and in Penzance more men were on the dole. Many of our customers cut their orders for milk and cream. Finally, we said farewell to our last milkman and my father delivered the milk himself. By 1936 when I was ten, I was aware not only of the need to economise, but also of the need not to exacerbate the tense family atmosphere.

My mother had a miserable time with me. Every year or two I had to be fitted with a new splint, and every week she had to take me to the orthopaedic clinic where the adhesions in my elbow were broken. This was achieved by three nurses pulling on my wrist and shoulder. I learnt not to cry because my mother suffered so. The upside was that I now have a very high pain threshold.

I still remember my pride when, without help, I tied my shoelaces into bows for the first time. I was often ill with asthma too. Sometimes I was in bed for seven or eight weeks at a time. On one occasion, I overheard the doctor (still the same one) saying to my mother, 'You must prepare for the worst.' But when I had recovered, he recommended the occasional herbal cigarette and taught me how to inhale!

I was given a Saturday penny every week by our cousins-in-law, the butchers across the road. They were forever sharpening their great knives as they gossiped all day long. My penny was riches. I went up to Merrifield's, the sweet shop at the top of the town, and bought a halfpenny's worth of bull's eyes, a farthing's worth of liquorice allsorts and a sherbet. My young 'uncles' were chapel, unlike us, and in the living room behind the shop hung a huge print of an eye with the legend, Lord Thou Seest Me. Despite this warning, they had a reputation in Penzance for chasing girls.

One of our great treats every week was the cinema, which I was first taken to at four years old, when most films were still silent. Concentrating on the subtitles helped me to learn to read. Penzance was the last cinema in Cornwall to show the latest feature film because the reels were taken from town to town until they reached us. Later, when sound cinema had replaced the silent movies, we had the news first, and then the feature film, and the evening ended with the national anthem, for which we all stood to attention, quivering with patriotism.

The Gaumont News was presented by a man with a commanding voice who barked the commentary; but at the end of the war, even he moderated his tone when pictures of the liberation of Belsen came on screen. If I close my eyes I can go straight back to that shabby picture house and recall those horrifying images: the corpses, the shock in the eyes of our soldiers, and the scarecrow survivors will always be with me. This is why I will never let an anti-Semitic remark go unchallenged.

When I was four years old, I started going to the local primary school, which was about a mile from the centre of Penzance. My elder sister, Peggy, had to walk with me for the whole of the first term, much to her annoyance. I loved her deeply and I admired her school friends too, but this feeling was not returned. They urged me to make my own friends instead of tagging along after them.

On my first day I met Miss Paul, a grey presence: grey hair, grey suit with a long skirt, a kind voice and, as I soon discovered, a loving heart. My sister explained to Miss Paul why my right arm, always above my head, was raised, not because I needed the lavatory or to ask a question.

We sat at little desks and were each given a coloured pencil and sheets of paper. Miss Paul wrote out the alphabet on the blackboard. This was old stuff to me – I had been taught to read by Peggy. I even knew one long word: expectorate. It was on an official notice in the public gardens: 'Gentlemen are forbidden to expectorate'.

I was preparing to demonstrate my knowledge when the little girl next to me said, 'My name's Elsie. What's yours?'

'Barbara,' I whispered. 'But I'm called Bobbie.'

'Well, Bobbie, you've got a red crayon and I've only got a blue one.'

'Yes.'

'I want your crayon.'

'But you've got your own, I want mine.'

'My da's a policeman.'

I didn't really understand, but I recognised a threat and gave her my crayon.

Miss Paul shushed us into silence and I turned my attention to the blackboard. Miss Paul never raised her voice, but within a year she turned a ragbag of undisciplined four-to-six-year-olds into attentive little girls – apart from me, that is. I was quite unable to keep quiet and my behaviour was wild. I fought and shouted and laughed noisily. I think I was a happy child, but I worried my parents and the school. At the end of the first year, my report was pretty bad and my mother went to see Miss Paul, who assured her that I would eventually learn self-discipline.

'She's going to do really well,' predicted Miss Paul. This

surprised my mother. She knew that Peggy was clever – very clever – but not I.

For the first time, I found my splint useful. If I was bored at school, I undid the leather strap which held my wrist up so that my arm hung at an apparently painful angle. I would tell my teacher, who would send me home. On one splendid occasion, I intervened when a bigger boy was bullying my brother. I swung my iron-clad right arm and broke his nose. Mummy worried about my behaviour and she worried about my asthma and eczema. When I wasn't boisterous, I was ill in bed. The family doctor prescribed rest and distraction. This led to a succession of neighbours calling with books and toys, and even a garrulous parrot. Nothing really worked. I would become suddenly ill for no apparent reason and recover quickly and just as mysteriously. Curiously, I recovered for ever when I left home…

I was six years old when I fell in love for the first time. Her name was Melvina Sowden. She lived with her mother, near the cattle market, in very poor circumstances. She was a quiet child with long, fair hair and blue eyes, which was very unusual in Penzance. We walked together to school and home again. I talked, and she laughed and looked mysterious. My parents were worried, partly because of the excessive nature of my love, and partly because they thought I would pick up Melvina's dreadful Cornish accent. It was many years before I realised that they had Cornish accents themselves.

My love affair ended, like so many of them when I was young, in heartbreak. Melvina's mother introduced her to little boys and I was no competition. My mother was relieved, as I then devoted more of my time to the piano and to singing lessons.

Looking back, my childhood seems to have been a succession of sunny days, on the cliffs or on the beach, in the sea or in the countryside, picking blackberries or watercress or taking home fish given to me by the friendly Newlyn fishermen. I went for walks with Geoffrey, my brother, when he was recovering from an operation for mastoiditis. Despite my poor health, my elementary school taught me well, and I had a good command of the three Rs, Reading, Writing and 'Rithmetic, plus some grasp of geography and history.

When we went to visit our grandmother in Newquay, my father found a new way to keep me quiet during the train journey: counting rabbits from the window – there were hundreds of them! I also played with friends on the promenade and watched the ladies playing bowls. One day, we saw posters for a competition at the local theatre. It was for children and they were asked to recite or sing. We went inside to find a packed theatre, and joined the queue for the stage. My friends decided to leave, but I decided to stay and recite a poem. I went forward on my own, whereupon one of the staff stopped me. 'You don't want to go on, do you?' He was looking at my arm. 'Yes please, I have a lovely little poem. Mummy likes it,' I replied, not understanding his objection. 'OK then, what's your name?' My name, Bobbie Hosking, was announced to the audience and I went to the middle of the stage, turned and faced them:

> I had a penny, a bright new penny,
> I took my penny to the market square.
> I wanted a rabbit, a little furry rabbit
> But they didn't have a rabbit anywhere there.

I was about six years old, going on seven, and I recited with emotion. The audience clapped. I was a success and I took home a prize, a small teddy bear. 'Bill,' my mother said, 'she stood alone on that stage. She didn't mind.' Apparently, my parents were amazed and moved, although I did not understand why.

In common with much of the town, we led a full religious life. We knelt by our beds morning and night to say our prayers, and went to church three times on Sunday at the parish church, St Mary's near the harbour. Geoffrey was a 'boat boy', which meant that, aged six, he wore a beautiful lace surplice and carried the silver vessel that held incense. I was in the choir. For some reason, Peggy seemed not to have been involved in any of our church activities and Sheila just tagged along.

I had a very comprehensive preparation for confirmation which involved staying for a week with the Sisters of the Epiphany in a large convent in Truro. The hardest thing for me was the rule of silence. At mealtimes one of the sisters read stories of the saints while we ate. The easiest part was the examination of our conscience. I was born with only a small amount of guilt and can usually forgive myself fairly easily for the general run of mortal sins.

The difficulty came some three years later when I started questioning some of the Creed. On Sundays, when we repeated it during Mass, I found that I could not accept 'the resurrection of the body'. For some months I just left this line out, but gradually other lines became difficult for me as well. I am now quite sure that all religion is man-made and I happily contemplate death as the end, full stop. But I still love the great psalms and singing hymns and I love the words of the prayer book: 'When the busy world is hushed and the fever of life is over.'

CHAPTER THREE

In 1936, when I was ten, it was time for the scholarship exam. If you passed you were eligible for the boys' or girls' grammar school, but poor children left school at fourteen whether they passed or failed. They found jobs on the land or at sea, went into service, or worked as shop assistants and errand boys. Families who could afford it kept their children at school longer and sent them to the grammar schools. But there were also two other girls' schools in Penzance, both boarding establishments. One was St Clare's, a Church of England school, the other West Cornwall, a Methodist school for the daughters of missionaries and other expats. This school offered two scholarships a year for local girls. When Peggy took the entrance exam, she did so well that headmistresses from several of the top schools in the south and west of England wrote to my mother offering my sister full boarding education. But my father refused to let her go. 'She has a perfectly good home here,' he argued. My mother was very disappointed and so was Peggy. She went to West Cornwall.

Now it was my turn. The examinations for West Cornwall School were held in a shining new, white building next to an old granite manor house high above the town. It was surrounded by the flower beds, shrubs, trees and lawns for which Cornwall is famous. I had sisterly advice from Peggy beforehand. 'When the mistress comes into the room,' she told me, 'ignore what the others do and stand up. Show her respect. And when she turns to leave, open the door for her, show her that you have good manners. Now when you see the list of questions take your time, choose the ones you know most about. And Bobbie, keep QUIET! No talking!'

I obeyed Peggy, and, as the only one to show politeness, I was rewarded with a surprised smile.

The summer moved on, and one Sunday after morning church my mother said, 'It's such a lovely day, Bobbie. Let's go for a walk, lunch is cold so it can wait.' We walked along the wide promenade while I talked. As we neared the Winter Garden Palais de Danse, we sat down to admire the view of Newlyn. Mummy took my hand. 'Bobbie darling, I have some news for you, but you must not get too excited. So take some deep breaths of sea air first.'

All my life I had been doing this. There was a stand of pine trees on the way to Mousehole where my mother often took me to breathe when the asthma was bad. 'Darling,' she said, after I had dutifully inhaled, 'you have passed the scholarship. You will be going to West Cornwall with Peggy in September.'

Eighty years on, and I still remember that moment: the place where we sat, and the kindness of my mother in telling me so gently that a huge door had opened in my life.

One sunny morning soon after, I was walking through our local gardens, famous for their luxuriant semitropical plants. I was looking forward to my first day at the new school. My mother had altered Peggy's uniform to fit me, which meant that my sister would have new clothes. I didn't mind. I was excited to be able to wear the chocolate-brown blazer, the tunic with a smart square neck, and the pale tussore silk blouse which proclaimed my superiority. I was happily whistling as I walked past huge rhubarb plants when I was stopped by one of the gardeners.

'Do you know, young lady,' he began,

> A whistling woman
> And a crowing hen
> Are neither fit
> For God nor men.

I didn't understand. He asked me to repeat the words after him. 'Remember them!' he said.

At home I asked my mother what the gardener meant. 'He meant that only boys should whistle,' she explained. 'The rhyme says that for a girl to whistle is as unnatural as for a hen to crow.'

'But it is natural for me to whistle. I like doing it.'

'Yes, my darling Bobbie. He is an ignorant man who should mind his own business. You go on whistling or, better still, singing, as much as you like.'

There was a special celebration tea for me, and my grandmother sent me ten pounds, a huge sum in 1936. However, there were two much more important changes. Encouraged by Peggy, I refused to wear the iron splint on my arm any longer. My only problem was that I couldn't salute because I couldn't raise my right arm above my shoulder, but I hoped I would never have to. The doctors reluctantly agreed that I could give up the splint. The other change was that I told my father he would never hit me again. He said I was now so good that there was no need.

The school was divided into four houses, each one competing with the others in both school work and sport. For bad behaviour or breaking the rules, a house was given a black mark. My house was St Aubyn's, the family name of our local squire who lived on St Michael's Mount. I wore my blue house brooch proudly, but no one was proud of me. One of the rules was no speaking in the corridors, but St Aubyn's was loaded with the highest number of black marks in the history of the school, thanks to my addiction to the spoken word.

'While we encourage a degree of spontaneity,' the head-mistress said at morning assembly, 'we also encourage self-control, and Barbara has none.'

Peggy was ashamed. I was ashamed.

'She is highly strung and delicate,' said my mother.

'She needs discipline,' said my father.

That I excelled at English and in walking the balance in our new high-tech gym counted for nothing. Slowly, I learnt to shut up, mainly in order to win a smile from our beautiful house captain, who was good at work and good at sport and with whom I was in love. This also embarrassed Peggy. 'A crush is one thing, but you go too far. Besides, she's a bit of a snob.'

Class awareness was strong at West Cornwall. Most of the boarders had chequebooks and wore beautiful silk blouses and well-cut skirts. One or two of them were, as Peggy said, a bit stuck-up, but most of them formed last-ing friendships with us. We scholarship girls spoke with a Cornish accent and were often teased. Once, when we were learning about eighteenth-century agriculture, I asked a question about farmer-earls. The mistress and class doubled up with laughter at my country 'r's, but my French accent was good. At lunchtimes we spoke only in French and I discovered that I have an ear like a parrot's and can often pick up foreign words with perfect pronunciation – nothing to do with intelligence, just a good ear.

I now spent my weekends bicycling around West Cornwall with my new friends, mostly local scholarship girls. We couldn't see over the huge granite boulders dug out of the bracken to make rough borders for the fields. Every now and then there would be a gap and we would look down on Penzance, with the dome of the bank building and the tower of St Mary's standing out and the arms of the Lizard and Mousehole circling the bay. In the evenings when I had finished my homework I played the piano. I loved the Edwardian ballads which were very popular then. They had names like 'Because' or 'Until' and manly baritones fiercely declared their undying love or grief in many Cornish drawing rooms. I pounded out 'The Indian Love Lyrics', a collection written by a British general's wife in the days of the Raj, and felt that 'Less than the Dust' totally expressed my emotions.

Despite the demands and pleasures of my first year at West Cornwall, I could not ignore the misery at home. Mummy's deeply worried expression was now permanent, and Daddy had been forced to sack his workmen. The dairy staggered on for a year before Daddy was made bankrupt.

Peggy explained to Geoffrey, Sheila and me that he did not have enough money to pay his debts. My brother and younger sister were too young, at nine and seven, to understand the full impact of this, but Peggy and I knew the seriousness of our position and the shame our parents felt.

'We will have to leave here,' Peggy explained.

'Perhaps Granny will help.' I was always optimistic.

'Not likely now. She could have helped earlier.'

'I'll ask her. She's always liked me.'

'Mummy won't let you.'

Granny was always a huge, unseen presence in our house. She was the only grandparent we had. Mummy spoke of her with sadness; Daddy, whose parents had died before we were born, with anger. Peggy and I took turns in spending summer holidays with her. Peggy's visits were short and full of arguments. Mine were longer. I liked Newquay and I liked Gran, and I encouraged her to reminisce. Her first husband, Mummy's father, had come wooing in a pony and trap, and tied red ribbons to his whip to show the world that he was courting. He came back from Alaska with enough money to buy a small farm. It was a love match, and they were happy until his sudden early death.

Sometimes, Gran would look sad, sigh and quote, 'Oh for the touch of a vanished hand, and the sound of a voice that is still.'

She loved poetry and gave me a sixpence for every poem

I learnt by heart. I have been grateful all my adult life for the poetry she embedded in my memory.

A couple of days after Peggy had explained to us about Daddy's troubles, we were told that Granny was coming from Newquay to see us. But where would she sleep? We had no spare bedroom. Granny would not be staying, Mummy said, she was coming for lunch and a talk.

And Granny's visit was indeed short. Each of the children was inspected, each was given a large white five-pound note about the size of a tissue, and then our parents were taken off to the solicitors. When they came home, Granny had already left for the Newquay train. We children were aware that decisions had been made. Mummy was looking less apprehensive but Daddy was just as fierce and sullen as ever.

He was blamed by Granny, who was an inspired shop-keeper and entrepreneur, for his bad management, but the decline of the dairy was not really his fault. Businesses were failing everywhere and he had never had any training on how to run a business when he was given the dairy.

A few weeks later at breakfast, we were told that we would be moving. 'We are going to live in St Mary's Ter-race,' Mummy announced, 'in a lovely granite house, at the top of the terrace. There is a garden at the side and we overlook the Morrab Gardens and St Michael's Mount.'

We did not have a removals firm to help us. We moved ourselves, piling all the big stuff, furniture and piano, into the van. We children carried smaller things down through the town, past inquisitive neighbours. Our former workmen came for the day to help. The piano went into the large first-floor sitting room, and I banged out a triumphant Czerny exercise, gazed at the Mount and rejoiced in the new life that was beginning for us all.

For us children it was a happy time. The school holidays had begun. It was a warm summer and Mummy took us every day to the beach. We would swim morning and afternoon and have a simple picnic for lunch. I was happy to stay with Mummy and the younger children, but Peggy, now thirteen and beginning to turn into a beautiful young woman, was bored. The boarders from school had all gone abroad to join their families so the day girls, like Peggy, hung around the many art galleries in Newlyn and St Ives.

It was not until much later that I learnt why Mummy spent all her days on the beach. She had no money, her clothes were old and she was avoiding her friends. The house where we lived was rented. Granny paid the rent but there was not much over. (I think it was then that I resolved never to be in debt. I always pay my bills by return. I have always bought everything outright and still do – from my first Mini to my last Audi A6. The only money I have ever owed was a mortgage on my first flat.)

Happily unaware of this at the time, the summer drifted on in a carefree haze of sunshine until 3 September 1939.

CHAPTER FOUR

Except for Daddy, all the family were in church when war was declared. The vicar placed a wireless on the edge of the pulpit and at eleven o'clock he turned it on and we heard the Prime Minister, Neville Chamberlain, announce that we were at war with Germany. The prayers for the country and the armed forces left most of the congregation in tears. They still remembered the slaughter of 1914–1918, the 'War to End All Wars', some twenty years earlier. And yet it was a beautiful day; everything seemed the same as we walked home through the quiet Sunday streets, and I wondered what 'being at war' meant.

For Daddy, the gathering crisis had already provided an unexpected escape from Penzance and unemployment. He had already joined the army earlier in 1939 and was now a commissioned officer, although he later told me that he would rather have been in the ranks. He was forty and his fellow officers were boys of twenty. It must have been difficult for him and I expect he was teased. For Mummy, ironically, the war brought about a much better life. She now had some money – a family allowance from the army – and, with Daddy away, the atmosphere at home improved greatly.

When he came home on leave for the first time, I made him walk past the bathing pool where there was a soldier with a rifle on sentry duty. When Daddy walked past, the soldier jumped to attention and I was filled with pride. We were all intensely patriotic. Peggy longed to join up, but she was only fifteen. 'I hope it will all be over before they need you,' my mother said.

It was Mummy's life that changed the most. To her surprise and delight, she was appointed a billeting officer for evacuees from London and other cities targeted by German bombs. For the first time in her life, like so many British women, she had paid employment and real decision-making responsibility. Cornwall was considered a safe area and so whole schools of pupils arrived with their smart uniforms and confident speech. My mother helped to solve problems and soothe ruffled feelings as country schools in West Penwith shared their facilities with these newcomers, one school using the premises in the mornings, the other in the afternoon. More importantly, my mother had to find accommodation for these children in the larger homes in and around Penzance – a job that required an enormous amount of tact.

When we first heard that evacuees were to arrive, the whole town crowded to the railway station. We were not allowed inside so we lined the high wall outside and stared through the railings. The train slowly rounded the curve of the bay and hissed to a stop. Clouds of white steam filled the roof and obscured the platform. As it cleared away we saw all these children, some very young, with name tags attached to their jackets and small gas masks slung around their necks.

Mummy was one of those who greeted the children and sorted out the homes which were taking them in. We were amazed and moved by the love and courage of parents who had trusted in the goodness of strangers to care for their daughters and sons, and it is a proud chapter in our Cornish history that their trust was rarely misplaced. Indeed, in the church school in Paul there is a plaque with the names of the evacuees. This was placed there by the families of East End children, most of them Jewish. They bonded with their Cornish foster parents, and often came back to visit when the war was over.

Although we escaped any major attacks by enemy aircraft, we were not wholly ignored. There was one real vulnerability in the area: the UK end of the transatlantic cable to the USA was housed in great rooms and tunnels in cliffs at Porthcurno. This was the main communication link between the two countries. It was often bombed, and planes offloaded any spare bombs on Penzance; waste not want not. At school, when the warning siren howled, we filed down into a large cellar under the stern eye of Miss Edwards, our maths mistress.

I once again broke the no talking rule.

'Go into the garden,' she commanded.

'But Miss Edwards, there's an air raid alert...'

'You should have thought of that before.'

Those were the days when girls' schools followed the Trojan creed of toughness, but Miss Edwards didn't always win her battles with me. When we were studying for the School Certificate maths exam she announced to the class, 'I know one girl who will fail,' and glared at me.

I told Mummy. 'We'll see about that,' she said.

One of our neighbours was a Professor Weinberg, who taught at the Camborne School of Mines. I spent many evenings in his terrifying, bearded presence, learning whatever maths he could reduce to a sixteen-year-old's level, and I passed the exams easily. Miss Edwards was speechless!

I ran the Public Affairs Group at school and, rather to the consternation of the headmistress, I invited writers and politicians to come and speak to us at West Cornwall.

When Phyllis Bottome was my guest, the whole school turned out to hear her. She had written *The Mortal Storm* and the novel had been turned into a film which we had all seen. It was about the impact of the Nazi Party on a middle-class German family and we wept over it. I spoke at the Cornwall Youth Parliament in Truro and, in 1942, when I was sixteen, I was asked by the BBC to take part in a broadcast debate at their Whiteladies Road studios in Bristol. This was the first time someone from my school had spoken on the radio.

Looking back, I realise that both my somewhat precocious cultural activities and a penchant for organising was an early portent of things to come much later. Meanwhile, the school was proud of me, and so were my parents, despite being deeply worried about my extreme politics. Ever a rebel, I had decided to become a Liberal in defiance of their Tory allegiance.

It was not long after this that Miss Killip, the headmistress, summoned me. She had decided that I should start Latin.

'Indeed, Barbara, I don't know why you haven't been studying Latin all along. You will need it for Oxford or Cambridge.'

By this time, my younger sister Sheila had joined me at West Cornwall School. She had a new school uniform, and the brown square-necked tunic and biscuit-coloured silk blouse suited her well. She was better behaved than I ever was, which certainly made her more popular with the staff. Geoffrey was at the Penzance County School for Boys, where his best subject was English. I didn't see much of Sheila at home because she was younger, but Geoff and I would go for long walks and talk about our futures. We both, it emerged, were nursing the same desire: to become writers.

My latter schooldays at West Cornwall were the happiest days of my mother's life. She was respected for her work and, although the job only lasted for three years, it gave her an awareness of skills which she hadn't known she possessed. Mummy used her money generously on little treats: a party dress for Sheila, fashionable trousers for Geoff, singing lessons for me, more pocket money for Peggy. She took me to tea at the Abbey Hotel on the harbour, in the poorest part of Penzance. Her friends, the clever Clifford family – he an architect, she a business-woman with a love of the arts – had rescued a beautiful eighteenth-century house, and indeed the whole street, from decay. When we went to the Abbey for cream teas, there might well have been a drunken artist from St Ives in the chaotic kitchen. Much later, it was bought by the model Jean Shrimpton and her husband, and the kitchen became quiet and orderly.

Sometimes we went to St Ives to look at the art galleries

and to buy seconds from the Leach Pottery. If she was lucky, Mummy would have a chat with Bernard Leach, he of a prayer in every pot.

My best friends at school were Mary Hichens and Eunice Williams, who both remained much-loved friends until the end of their lives. Mary was also a scholarship girl who lived in Newlyn, and her father was a plumber who had worked in South Africa, as so many Cornishmen did when times were hard. He brought back a South African wife who gave him five pretty daughters. Eunice lived with her grandparents in St Just. Her parents divorced when she was very young and she had never known her father. Her mother lived in London and occasionally appeared at school functions with handsome men. She was beautiful with a deep, upper-class voice, unlike her daughter who spoke like me and Mary. She appeared in a cloud of Je Reviens, called me darling, and introduced us to the Marquess of Milford Haven and other admirers of hers. She gave her daughter an MG sports car for her seventeenth birthday. Mary and I were taken on terrifying drives around Zennor while Eunice learnt to change gear. Sometimes Eunice's mother took us away to Exeter for weekends. We stayed at the Clarence Hotel and I learnt how to behave in an expensive dining room.

Although we were too young to be involved in active war work, we longed to help in some way, so when we heard of work in the fields at weekends we eagerly volunteered.

We spent our summer holidays working for local farmers. One hot sunny day, we were weeding cabbages when we heard a plane approaching. We turned to wave when, to our astonishment, it opened fire. It was the first time we had heard a machine gun, or seen the dark markings of a German plane. We dived into the hedge and watched as it flew off in the direction of St Michael's Mount. We learnt later that sunbathers on the beach at Marazion had been machine-gunned, two had been wounded, and the plane had been one of several which had unsuccessfully bombed the cable station earlier that day.

In 1942, Peggy had achieved her ambition and joined the Women's Royal Naval Service. She was seventeen and a half, the earliest possible age for entry, long before women were integrated into the Royal Navy. In those days, after basic naval training, most women were assigned to the clerical or catering departments. Peggy, with her starred School Certificate, was sent to learn meteorology on an airfield in Northern Ireland. She was young, healthy, beautiful and intelligent, and looked splendid in her uniform.

Six months later she was dismissed. She was pregnant.

My father was given leave to come home for this crisis. He was in the worst rage we had ever known.

'She can't live here. I won't allow it. She has brought disgrace on the family.'

'But Bill, where can she go? We must look after her. She is our daughter.'

The tears and the shouting went on while Sheila and Geoffrey were sent to bed, and I watched in misery. Finally, the only possible decision was made and I was sent down to the railway station to meet her.

'Have you come to greet the Prodigal Daughter, Bobbie?' She attempted a brave smile, but we were soon both in tears. I told her about the rows at home and the accusations of disgrace.

'He's a fine one to talk!' she said, with a flash of anger.

Until then I had known nothing of my father's infidelities, and was shocked by Peggy's words. For the first time I understood Mummy's sadness. I came to realise that she had hinted at Daddy's behaviour, but I had been too ignorant to realise that.

Peggy told us about John that night. He was a handsome, young officer in the Fleet Air Arm. They loved each other and intended to marry when they could, but he already had a wife. Another explosion from Daddy. But, eventually, they did marry, had six fine children and lived happily together until Peggy's death.

CHAPTER FIVE

It was in 1943 that the American soldiers arrived. We were shocked when they marched into Penzance because they moved so silently. In our experience, there was always the sound of heavy boots when our soldiers marched and drilled, but these columns of men moved like ghosts in their rubber-soled boots. We decided that they couldn't possibly be very good fighting men. Our opinion had to be revised when the Royal Inniskilling Fusiliers were also stationed near Penzance: the fights between the two regiments at the Palais de Danse on Saturday nights were spectacular.

At the end of the war, Mary, Eunice and I heard that one of our school friends, Heather Williams from Newlyn, was going to marry an American soldier and move to the United States. His parents had emigrated to America from Newlyn years earlier, so Heather – one of the first GI brides – was actually marrying the boy next door.

We knew that Heather would be terribly homesick for Cornwall as she made a new life so far away, so we bought her a granite replica of Bishop Rock Lighthouse as a wedding present. It stood some three feet high. It was very heavy so it was either the lighthouse or the luggage and we were saddened to learn that our gift found a home in the window of her parents' home in Newlyn, proudly displayed for all the neighbours to see!

Just before the summer holidays in 1944, the headmistress, Miss Killip, sent for me. Throughout my schooldays I had spent much miserable time waiting outside her door, guilty of something in my teacher's eyes, my own eyes and in the eyes of passers-by. This time I waited with the confidence of a sixth-former, and a school leaver.

'Come.'

I entered the familiar room, high-ceilinged, book-lined, with generous bow windows looking out past a luxuriant Cornish garden to the sea.

Miss Killip asked most kindly after Peggy ('such a naturally clever girl') and my parents. I answered politely, aware that the gossip of the town rarely penetrated the walls of the school, which lived like an alien colony on the outskirts.

'As you know, Barbara, your exam results were disappointing. Excellent marks for English language and literature, good marks for history and French, but abysmal marks for Latin. I know you only started Latin in the sixth form, but a girl of your calibre should have sailed through. As we have always said, learning has been easy for you. You have never had to work hard and so you didn't apply yourself to Latin.'

I agreed that I hadn't worked hard enough.

'Now, Barbara, you need Latin for Oxford and Cambridge, and it doesn't do for a girl like you to leave us without matriculation.' Her expression was softer than I'd ever seen it. 'Therefore,' she continued, 'we have decided to renew your scholarship for another year, so that even if you don't go to university you will leave here properly equipped for life.'

She was kind. The school was kind. I looked at her and knew that I couldn't begin to explain why I so desperately needed to leave home. Miss Killip's fastidious style, her well-kept hands and her beautiful shoes were light years from Peggy's baby and my father's bankruptcy.

I thanked her warmly and explained that I was impatient to begin earning.

Her last words to me were a reference to my fatal facility. 'You must learn how to work,' she said.

I didn't tell my parents of the offer to renew my scholarship. It would have meant another row. Instead, I wrote to every newspaper editor in Cornwall and Devon asking for work, any work. The war was ending, and even if an editor were prepared to take on a girl – which was pretty unlikely – she would be competing against the men coming home. There was no contest. Some of the rejections were quite kind and suggested that, for a start, I should learn shorthand and typing.

Miss Wesley's secretarial school was the only one in Penzance. Strong men lowered their voices when they spoke of Miss Wesley. She was hugely respected – tall, well-built, a deep voice with confident vowels. A voice accustomed to command and to be heard across the family fields. She had founded her school in the 1930s and it was very profitable. She knew about business, and some of the smarter townsfolk sought her out discreetly for advice. Miss Wesley had a partner in the school, Miss Drew, who did most of the teaching. She wore soft woollen dresses, little pink scarves and shoes that emphasised her small feet. She fined the students if they made mistakes, and the money went into a box for the People's Dispensary for Sick Animals.

I knew Miss Wesley slightly and decided to go and see her. She met me in her study, which housed a huge desk, flanked by large books which I later learnt were dictionaries and legal books. I suppose there were windows, but I don't remember them. I said I wanted to learn shorthand and typing – and book-keeping, she added. I explained that we had no money since my father's bankruptcy, and

I could tell from her expression that she clearly knew all about it.

'If you will teach me for nothing,' I said, 'I will work for you for nothing.'

A few moments silence. Then, looking thoughtful, she said, 'I will have to discuss this with my partner, Miss Drew. It would be a departure from our usual policy ... would we draw up a contract? ... what timescale are we thinking of...?' She looked at me intently through her large spectacles. 'You want to be a journalist. Difficult for a girl. We'll see.'

Miss Wesley then told me about some of the work they were doing – a novel by Storm Jameson, annual accounts for half the town. I went back to see her a week later.

'Miss Drew has suggested, and I agree, that we should give you six months to see how you progress,' she said. 'By then, you might almost be helpful to us. You play the piano so you'll take to the keyboard. Please give my regards to your mother. By the way, does she know that you have come to see me?' I confessed that she did not, that this was my own idea.

I loved Miss Wesley's. Every day, I left my family problems behind me and entered the order and calm of focused lives where, it seemed, nothing ever went wrong. We went there to work so that we could earn our own living. The other pupils were grammar-school girls I hardly knew.

Their sisters and brothers already had low-level jobs in Barclays Bank or Boots, but they aspired to senior secretarial positions. With the arrogance of youth, I felt superior to all of them. I had been to the best school, after all; I wasn't going to be a secretary, I was going to be a writer.

There was a pleasing logic to shorthand and I enjoyed learning it; soon, I was able to start taking dictation. Similarly, my fingers skipped along the keys under Miss Drew's approving eye as she played 'Half a pound of tuppenny rice, half a pound of treacle...' on a gramophone, while we typed in unison to the beat. More than speed, though, our typing goal was accuracy. It was important to be accurate because of the difficulty of correcting work, especially with three or four carbon copies, while a legal document had to be absolutely accurate or it was not legally valid.

Fortunately, Miss Wesley and Miss Drew liked me and seemed to enjoy my company but, above all, they trusted me to be vigilant in checking work. I stayed on at the end of the day after the others had left. Miss Drew gave me tea and cakes and told me about their early life and about how they had once bicycled to London and back. Then we would begin the checking and they started paying me a salary. It was here that I first really learnt about proper work. They worked hard. They had a reputation for beautifully produced documents and manuscripts, and assignments came in from everywhere, often novels and poetry as well as business reports.

Miss Drew explained that I had to look out for grammar, spelling and punctuation. We took turns in reading out loud and she asked me to begin: 'Chapter Three. Inverted commas … Capital 'H' Hello, comma, young capital 'S' Susan, full stop … Inverted commas … Space … Capital 'H', he looked at her quizzically … full stop.'

'Have I spelt quizzically correctly?'

'Yes, Miss Drew.'

Within a year I was employed full time. My father was still in the army. Peggy and John had moved away and had more children. I learnt to my disbelief that my darling elder sister loved everything about babies, from being pregnant to teaching them to walk and talk. That was when she was really happy. My mother was happier too. Her worries had decreased. The two youngest children were doing well at school, and, with a smaller family to look after, she had time for herself – time to visit art galleries, time to sing with the local choral group, time to enjoy herself. As the war drew to its end, civil life started up again.

At about this time, Miss Wesley called me into her office.

'There is a vacancy for a really good secretary. It's in the Isles of Scilly, secretary to the Town Clerk,' she said. 'We don't want to lose you, Barbara, dear, but Miss Drew and I felt we had to bring it to your attention because it's an excellent position. The council has the status of county council and your salary would be four pounds, ten shillings a week.' That was a high salary in 1945, and I hoped my face didn't betray my disbelief. 'Of course,' Miss Wesley went on, 'we do not wish you to leave us; in fact we had considered making you a junior partner.'

Freedom at last.

I thanked them both very sincerely for all their kindness to me. I owed them so much, and I look back in gratitude and affection for those two special ladies.

CHAPTER SIX

In the Isles of Scilly, secretary to the Town Clerk was an important position. As a county council, salaries were high. Out of my four pounds, ten shillings a week, I paid my landlady, Mrs Gendall, two pounds ten for full board, so I had two pounds 'pocket money' every week. I was rich! In 1945, many families in Cornwall lived on less, and I relished being able to smoke Player's Perfectos Finos.

The Town Clerk was an Old Etonian, a lawyer and a bachelor. We discussed painting, literature and poetry and he lent me books. The deputy Town Clerk was recently demobbed from the RAF. He had won the DFC. I was inordinately proud of him, and he was embarrassed. Both men rejoiced in the Christian name of Roland; I came to think of them as Roland One and Roland Two.

Our offices were in the town hall. The walls of the main

room in which I worked were decorated with flintlock rifles, pikes and beautifully painted Victorian truncheons. My work was not arduous. Although we ranked as a county council, this was really an administrative convenience and was usually undemanding. Roland One also provided private legal advice to local people, usually concerning wills. I earned extra money, a small second income, for typing these, copying chunks out of textbooks and displaying them importantly with many capitals and much underlining.

I soon acquired a third income when I learnt that the local stringer for *The Cornishman*, the Penzance newspaper, who had been reporting local news for many years, was tired of the job. The editor accepted my first stories and gave me a contract at a penny a line. I was nothing if not enthusiastic, and from then on he was bombarded with news from the islands. Births, marriages and deaths, or hatches, matches and dispatches, as we journalists called them, were easy. The editor wanted names and I supplied them. At the end of the week when the plane brought the newspapers, I added up my earnings using a ruler, the marks on which coincided with the lines of the printed columns.

An additional news source appeared when my landlady took on another lodger. Victor managed St Mary's airport, a wind-battered landing strip near the cliffs where small planes and helicopters landed. One night all the cars on the island, eight of them, were recruited to light the air-strip for an emergency take-off: Mrs Trembath was having her baby and there were complications. That was a front-page story in *The Cornishman*.

Victor alerted me if anyone important was coming to St Mary's. When a 'Distinguished Person' arrived, the press – me – was ready and waiting to ask for a few words. Sometimes I was able to have a longer and more formal talk, as when I heard that the writer G. B. Stern was arriving. I turned up early and humbly requested a full interview. I knew that she came from a cosmopolitan Jewish family, and had written some very successful plays as well as her dozens of novels. Miss Stern invited me to tea at her hotel and gave me a long interview, then asked to see what I had written before I sent it off. I suspected that a real professional journalist would not have agreed, but I was much too in awe of her to object. She wrote me an encouraging letter, returned my piece unaltered, and wished me good fortune.

On Saturdays Victor and I, together with Stella, the local schoolmistress, took turns to bring a bottle of wine over to Roland Two's house. We listened on old 78 rpm records to Tchaikovsky and Beethoven, and we composed sonnets. We obviously thought of ourselves as the local intelligentsia.

But we also wrote some rude limericks:

An old poultry keeper asserted
I am not really perverted
But a Rhode Island Red
Can be great fun in bed
And frustration so cheaply averted

That was one of mine.

There was always something to report from the islands, but on Christmas Day 1945 we had a big national story. That morning, the BBC, as always at Christmas, broadcast a special and inclusive programme that brought together listeners in the Commonwealth, the Empire and all our troops serving overseas, through radio link-up. The programme was transmitted to and from all over the world, and this year there was one from our very own Bishop Rock lighthouse.

A famous broadcaster, Edward Ward – the Dimbleby of his day – was landed on the Rock with transmitting equipment. On Christmas Day the world, or at least the British world, tuned in to greetings from remote corners of the globe. The broadcast went well, and the three lighthouse keepers, encouraged by Edward Ward, gave our Christmas greetings to the world. We were all very proud that the Scillies had been chosen that year, but by nightfall the weather had closed in and the Isles of Scilly, together with Bishop Rock lighthouse and its distinguished guest, who also happened to be the future Lord Bangor, were cut off (as was, of course, the only journalist around to gather all this news!).

It was six weeks before the sea was calm enough to send a boat to rescue Edward Ward. By then, the lighthouse keepers had had enough of looking after their charge, charming and grateful though he was. He even bought one of the rugs they used to make to sell when they came ashore. I was thrilled to be given a by-line in the *Western Morning News* and a paragraph in the *Daily Mail*.

During the first weeks of that December, the Rolands, both keen pianists, decided to play a concert piece for two pianos at the town hall's Christmas party. They knew that I could also play, so for many hours during December, I went downstairs with one or other Roland to rehearse Handel's 'The Arrival of the Queen of Sheba'. I still remember both parts of this famous duet but, alas, am too long out of practice to play a note of it.

In those days, all the Isles of Scilly were owned by Major Arthur Dorrien-Smith. He lived on Tresco, where he improved the already beautiful sub-tropical gardens. We were always on our best behaviour when he visited. He had long meetings with the Town Clerk and then we would all assemble for drinks. He usually brought gifts: a brace of pheasant for the Town Clerk, two rabbits for the deputy and half a dozen eggs for me. Today, the late major's family owns only the island of Tresco, on which he created another Eden.

Apart from news gathering, swimming and dancing in the town hall on Saturday nights, I became friends with Stella the schoolmistress, a good-looking woman a bit older than me and much more serious. She followed the philosophy and educational practices of Rudolf Steiner. We had long discussions on nature and nurture and 'The Meaning of It All' while sunbathing on the granite rocks at Peninnis. I was attracted to her, but would have been appalled if she had had any idea of how I felt. This was my guilty secret. I couldn't understand my feelings. There was no one in Penzance I could talk to and certainly no one on the islands. Then Michael arrived.

Michael was employed in the helicopter station in Penzance and had been sent to St Mary's to help out during the summer months. Nowadays I would have thought him a bit camp, but back then I just thought he was rather theatrical. His uniform suited his tall, slim build and dark, handsome Cornish face. He was, to my knowledge, the first homosexual I had met, and we soon became friends and confidants. He was, of course, very discreet. Both the law and his employers would have punished him if they had known. He lived most happily with an older man in Penzance, where they were regarded as two bachelors and were invited everywhere. For the first time I was able to talk openly about my feelings. I loved being with men as friends, but I didn't want a boyfriend or marriage or motherhood.

'There are hundreds of girls like you around,' Michael assured me. 'We must find one for you. When are you coming to Penzance?'

I was usually reluctant to go home at weekends, but this was different. I was doubtful about Michael's confidence, though. I knew most of the young women in Penzance and they were certainly all wholeheartedly looking for Mr Right and babies. Nevertheless, off I went the following weekend and met up with Michael.

'We'll try the railway station,' he said. 'It works for us boys sometimes.'

This made me even more dubious, but Michael was my only navigator in this strange new world. If Penzance railway station was the answer, I had better go along with it.

We stood at the top of the iron steps inside the entrance, from where Michael surveyed the platforms.

'There, look! We'll try her!' He pointed to where a land girl in her regulation uniform of green jumper and fawn breeches sat on a bench, smoking. 'Go on, Bobbie, ask her for a light.'

I held back. What on earth was I doing?

'Go on. That's what I would do,' encouraged Michael.

So I did. I approached her with my best smile and met

a weather-beaten face with no answering friendliness. She lit my cigarette and turned away. I went back to Michael.

'Ask her if she's meeting someone, or waiting for a train.'

I swallowed hard and went up to her again.

'What do you think you're playing at?' she shouted. Her London voice was harsh. 'Go away before I call the police, you silly girl.'

We fled. 'Perhaps it's different for girls. We'll try again later,' said Michael, attempting to console me.

Oh, no, we won't, I thought, feeling hugely embarrassed and very stupid. There might be some kindred soul somewhere but not, I concluded, in Cornwall.

I concentrated on enjoying the open-air life of the islands in the summer, swimming and picnicking with my friends. And indoors, particularly in the winter and long before the fashion for book groups, we read and discussed our favourite authors. And my last summer on the island brought a different and exciting injection of culture: the arrival of a touring theatrical company.

They booked the town hall, below our offices, and I was instructed to help them with whatever they needed, which was mostly props, whether a hatbox or a fortune-teller's crystal ball. My reward was a part in *Night Must Fall*, a thriller by Emlyn Williams in which I was the district nurse, and another in Noël Coward's *Blithe Spirit* as the maid – a key role which I played, or rather overplayed, passionately. After this unexpected experience, it became clear to me that however my life turned out it would not include a future on the stage.

My local journalism, however, flourished. By this time, my earnings from *The Cornishman* were some four rulers' worth a week and my savings increased. It was an idyllic life, but it was not enough. I wanted to be a real writer with real writer friends. By 1947, it was high time I started. Surely there would be something for me in London.

I was twenty-one and felt that hundreds of golden opportunities were passing me by. With no one to advise me, I decided I would find my own way of moving on. I broke the news to Roland One, my sympathetic boss, who was not at all surprised. He knew I wanted a career, and wished me well. My head girl at school had gone to London earlier to live with a cousin. I was able to get in touch with her, and she found me a bedsit in Swiss Cottage.

There were farewell parties and a weekend at home. My mother was looking after Peggy's baby, a fair-haired boy called David, while Peggy and John looked for a farm they could rent. My sister Sheila had begun training as a nurse at our local hospital. She did well, and became a theatre nurse at the big teaching hospital in Bristol before marriage to an oil executive took her off to Sarawak. Geoffrey had been accepted as a reporter on the local paper. Later he moved to the *Falmouth Packet*, and after a year or so he was offered a job on the *Manchester Guardian*. He turned it down. How could anyone live in Manchester? he asked with typical Cornish ignorance. I would have lived there on bread and water for a chance to work for *The Guardian*. I said goodbye to my siblings without sadness. I wished I could make my mother's life happier, but I couldn't.

On a Monday morning in spring, the great train, billowing steam, howled its way out of Penzance and along the beach to Marazion. I watched St Michael's Mount recede as we turned inland. The train gathered speed and raced up through Cornwall to my new life. The war had been over for a year, I was twenty-one years old, and I was on my way to seek fame and fortune in London.

PART II

GATEWAYS

CHAPTER SEVEN

My bedsit was up three flights of stairs in a terraced house in Lancaster Grove, Swiss Cottage. It had all I needed: a bed, two armchairs, a sofa, a big table and a kitchen recess with hot and cold water. There was a communal bathroom across the corridor shared with two others, a middle-aged secretary and a young jazz musician. They told me where to shop and how to get around on the bus and Tube.

They also told me about our landladies, Daisy and Rose. They were Jewish. They were sisters. The first was true; the second – as I would learn – was not. Daisy and Rose were as foreign and exciting as everything else I encountered. They were both good-looking in different ways. Daisy was tall and dark with black flashing eyes and dark skin; Rose shorter, fairer, quieter. They spoke with strong East End accents and were quick to laugh and tease each other and their tenants. Although they were streetwise, they struck me as amazingly ignorant: they knew nothing of Cornwall and had never heard of the Isles of Scilly!

I had met them only briefly when I arrived and they explained the rules of the house. I soon found that actually there were no rules. Perfect. And Swiss Cottage was everything I wanted it to be, full of foreign-looking young people and older couples who had fled from Germany with the rise of Hitler. Then there were the food shops, strange and wonderful to me; I loved Grodzinski's, the Polish–Jewish bakery and I loved the delicatessens and the cafes and restaurants, Chinese, Polish, Jewish. I wanted to try them all immediately.

But first, I had to get a job, and the landladies suggested I look in the *Evening Standard*. If I hadn't been so ignorant myself, I would have tried to find a secretarial job in publishing, but I was too much of a country girl to plan properly. The *Standard* advertised hundreds of typing jobs, so I got going on the communal phone in the hall for a couple of hours, and managed to set up three interviews for the following day. The men who interviewed me seemed surprisingly uneducated but they were pleasant, and by the end of the day I had three job offers. Of the three, I chose the headquarters of the Odeon and Gaumont cinema chains. Their offices were in Wardour Street, and I'm sure the idea of working in Soho, let alone the film industry, influenced my choice.

The typing pool was a large room where some fourteen young women sat behind large typewriters. The supervisor, a middle-aged survivor of the typing pool herself, looked after us and checked our work. The rules were strict and – as I would realise some years later – the office treated women as second-class citizens. Boys and women had to clock in and out each day, while men were free to come and go without supervision. Only men could smoke. You could talk quietly to your neighbours but real conversations and laughter were discouraged. Everything was so different from my previous life with my Old Etonian boss, but I didn't mind. I knew it wouldn't last.

I typed standard business letters for spotty youths with amazing glottal stops, and listened to the young women around me who were all marking time before they found Mr Right and got married. My wish to have a career rather than a wedding struck them as incomprehensible.

I bought my lunches at a delicatessen across the road, where everything was new to me and delicious. I might as well have been in a foreign country. The smoked salmon bagels with cream cheese were my particular favourite. 'How do you pronounce bagel?' I asked. 'How do you pronounce challah?' The elderly man who usually served me was amused by my interest.

'It depends where you're from,' he said. 'If you are from Poland, it's bygel. If you're from Spain, it's baygel.'

So I learnt about the different groups of Jews – and their snobbery. The Jews from Eastern Europe who had come here with nothing, and the grand Sephardic Jews from Spain.

I asked Daisy where her family had come from.

'Russia,' she replied. 'They thought they'd reached America when they landed in Liverpool. Why do you ask?'

I explained about the bagels.

'Do you like Jewish food?'

'I don't know. I love what I buy in Wardour Street.'

We were gradually becoming friendly, and she invited me to join her and Rose for supper one evening. We had cold fillets of fish which had been dipped in beaten egg, a thin coating of flour and matzo meal before frying. I thought I knew everything about fish, but I had never had cold fried fish before. It was delicious. Rose told me about her family, who had a market stall in Petticoat Lane, and I told them about Cornwall and its history. Every Saturday night they dressed in their best slacks and went clubbing. I had a free pass to all Odeon and Gaumont cinemas so my Saturday nights were spent seeing new films in Leicester Square.

One day at work, I encountered a young woman in the ladies who did not work with us. We talked, and she was clearly not typing pool material. Her name was Rene and she was the deputy editor of the Odeon and Gaumont house magazine, *The Circle*. We had lunch together, and it turned out that her education was similar to mine but, wisely, she had not learnt shorthand and typing. We became friends, and are still friends today. Rene was warm and generous, full of energy and wit. That was over seventy years ago and, while her energy is a bit less now and the wit a bit darker, her generosity is as warm as ever.

Rene's boss, Peter – a university-educated RAF pilot until a couple of years previously – edited *The Circle*. Rene, who covered for Peter when he went off to a drinking club, introduced us. He was welcoming and interested in my background. I often talked with him when I collected Rene for lunch. When she left for a brilliant career as an advertising copywriter at J. Walter Thompson, I was given her job.

No more typing pool! I was a full-time writer at last. I joined the National Union of Journalists and spent lunchtimes reading old copies of *The Circle*, which was compiled for all the staff at our hundreds of cinemas. We wrote about films, film stars and usherettes. We wrote about re-opening cinemas which had been bombed and we designed glossy commemorative programmes for the opening ceremonies. Peter laughed at my purple prose, and enjoyed teasing me. Just right for Bradford, he would say.

He smoked incessantly and his hands shook. He was generous in his criticism of my work, correcting, explaining. Sometimes we wrote slogans for banners that were hung across the entrance to cinemas, or for huge posters. My best effort, for a torrid love story, was 'She wasn't a wife for much of her life but she was a wow as a widow!' Too long, said Peter. But it was used.

I went to Pinewood and Ealing to report on films being made there, including *The Man in the White Suit* with Alec Guinness, and *Hotel Sahara*, where I was much impressed when the studio doors were locked while the sultry Yvonne Dc Carlo danced! I had a small expense account and no longer had to sign in and out of the building with the boys. But I wasn't a senior woman, I was an honorary man.

As friendship with my landladies progressed, they told me that they were not sisters but cousins, and had decided to live together when they left school. But there was more to their statement than I initially grasped.

'We didn't ever want to get married,' I was told with great emphasis.

'Neither do I,' I replied, feelingly.

'No, we thought you didn't,' they responded, with even greater emphasis. Could they possibly mean that they were…? I could hardly think the word let alone say it. They looked at me expectantly. 'No. I've no time for all that marriage and motherhood.' Daisy and Rose visibly relaxed.

'We're going clubbing tomorrow night. Would you like to come? Wear your smart slacks, we're going to Chelsea.'

The following evening we drove in Rose's small Austin to a club called the Gateways in Chelsea. 'You are queer, aren't you?' they asked as we went down the steps to a hidden door.

'Oh, yes,' I said, wondering if this was indeed so, if it showed in some way, and what it meant.

Daisy bought me a drink at the club's bar, which was manned by an amazingly masculine-looking woman, and I looked around me. There were some forty women in the room, mostly young, many of them dancing to the music that had greeted us. Someone asked me to dance, and asked my name. Her voice could have been that of one of my school friends, and I relaxed a little. I bought Rose and Daisy drinks and they each danced with me. We left fairly early.

'Well? What do you think? Did you like it, Bobbie?'

I thanked them and said I'd enjoyed the evening, but it was difficult to tell them how I really felt, because I found it difficult to know myself. I wished I had a friend that I could talk to about it.

At lunch on Monday, I took a chance and told Rene. Her response was amazingly understanding. I told her I was not at all sure that I had anything in common with the young women I'd met at the Gateways, and that I certainly felt no extra rapport with my landladies. Their lives and tastes were too different for us ever to be really close friends. I seemed to be more mixed up now than I was before.

Rene advised me to stop worrying. 'At least you now know that there are girls like you around, and some of them go to clubs. It's an advance.'

That much was true. I'd certainly moved on from accosting a stranger on Penzance station! I took Rene's advice and went to the Gateways sometimes with my landladies and met an extraordinary range of women, from prostitutes to university lecturers. I danced with them all, memorably with Jeanette, a plumpish nineteen-year-old prostitute from Yorkshire with a beautiful smile, and as wholesome as freshly baked bread. She was an only child, and as I grew to know her she told me her story: of the father who had raped her from the age of twelve, and of the mother who found out when Jeanette was sixteen and threw her out of the house. She lived entirely outside the law. Everything was paid for in cash, and a friendly shopkeeper in the Edgware Road, who sold cigarettes and sweets, became her banker. She took him her earnings every day and he kept her money safe, giving her cash when she wanted it. Jeanette had two pieces of luck, I reflected: she was not run by some petty criminal pimp, and the shopkeeper was honest. One evening, she appeared with a black eye; on another with a cut lip. When I asked her what happened, she laughed it off and changed the subject.

In 1949 there were very few places where gay women could go to enjoy each other's company without alarming Mrs Grundy. Many of the women at the club were careful to keep their private lives private and were reluctant to trust newcomers. However, I gradually made friends, and today I still have two friends that I first met there.

Most of the time I was focused on work, but I sometimes went to parties in big flats in Kensington and Baker Street, much smarter than my bedsit. It was at a party in Gloucester Place that my life changed direction again. It was where Chris Athey lived. I had met her at the Gateways; she was a lecturer at Froebel, and we became close friends. I well remember the taste of her delectable Swedish meatballs, but, more significantly, I remember her authoritative voice saying, 'You are wasting your life. You have a fine mind. You need more education!'

I thought I had done quite well in that department already – pre-university was not bad, while, as a newcomer to London with no one to help me, I had found an interesting job which was not too badly paid. I believed I had my foot firmly on the ladder.

'You must come and see me,' said Chris, brooking no argument. 'We must talk.'

So I did, and she told me about Hillcroft, an adult

education college for women in Surbiton, sometimes referred to by the students as 'the college of the second chance'. Students were accepted entirely on their ability to study. Hillcroft was residential, and in my case it would all be paid for by the London County Council. It seemed too good to be true but it was. I couldn't resist the prospect of a year of study, and thought with regret of my headmistress's offer of help to go on to Oxford or Cambridge.

When I met the principal of the college, Mrs Dyson, she told me about the suffragettes who had founded Hillcroft. They were women of leisure who had never had to work, and who met young working-class women as equals for the first time during the First World War. Until then, their communication with their servants would hardly have gone beyond discussing menus, but they realised that the working women were intelligent and that it was lack of education which held them back. They raised money from Gordon Selfridge of the department store and Mr Wall of Wall's Sausages among others, bought a large property and, in 1919, founded Hillcroft.

I loved it there. Once again, I was with a mixed group of women: a trades unionist from Manchester who developed a love of Socrates; two Abyssinian relatives of King Haile Selassie; and many half-educated young women who soaked up lectures like sponges. The year 1951 was a wonderfully indulgent year for me, concentrating on the English novel with the friendly help of Cambridge-educated Elisabeth Gibson.

In the early summer, one of the more political students asked me if I would like to attend a peace conference in Sheffield. It would mean roughing it with sleeping bags in little tents, but we would meet famous people and our views would be heard. What followed was an important political lesson for me.

We were greeted by totally committed young men who organised us throughout the weekend. They were not left-wing; they were hard left: communists, Trotskyists and, mostly, Socialist Workers Party members. They didn't want to discuss politics; they wanted to recruit us. All I remember now are the songs we learnt: 'The Voice of the City Is Sleepless', 'Go Home Yankee', 'Bau auf, Bau auf Frei Deutsches Jugen' and 'The Internationale'. We were told Picasso was there, but I certainly didn't see him. Above all, I remember the horror of wriggling into a tiny tent and trying to sleep. I vowed never to accept an invitation to go camping ever again. More significantly, I also learnt that the hard left were not democratic.

The only sadness during the year was the death of my grandmother. She had always been kind and encouraging to me, and I would miss her sharp comments on everything from the Conservative Party to the Church of England and the price of food. She had been contemplating taking a fourth husband when she died suddenly. In her will, Granny left her house and estate in a trust to my mother 'so that your father can't get hold of anything', I was told later. She left Peggy, Geoffrey and Sheila £1,000 each and she left me £5,000 and her jewellery, because of my 'poor arm'. This was a very handsome sum in 1951.

As my happy year reached its close, Mrs Dyson asked me about my politics. 'Liberal,' I replied, like the good Cornishwoman I was, and am.

'Oh dear, I thought you were more left than that,' she said. 'I would so like one of our students to become an MP and the best way is through the Labour Party, even though they're still fairly misogynistic. But they're better than the others. I suppose you wouldn't consider...?'

I thought about it. I had developed a passion for politics, and had spent many evenings with the Manchester trades unionist discussing the great reforms which the Labour government was introducing, but I was not a paid-up member of any political party. I decided to see whether Mrs Dyson actually could get me a job with the Labour Party.

And indeed she could. And did.

CHAPTER EIGHT

In 1952, I was offered a job by Morgan Phillips, the general secretary of the Labour Party. I phoned my mother in Cornwall with the news that I would be working at Transport House. 'Oh dear,' she said, 'I hope it's nothing to do with the buses.' I reassured her that it was not, and gave her my new address. I had given up my bedsit in Swiss Cottage when I went to Hillcroft, and was now the proud possessor of a bedsit in Islington. Parts of Islington were, and are, very fashionable, but not in the Holloway Road where I lived. I was definitely with the workers.

My first job with the Labour Party was not exactly a springboard to the House of Commons. Once again, I dived back into a typing pool, although this time it was more like a small classroom. Three rows of four desks faced a platform on which was placed a huge wooden chair resembling a throne. It was from here that Ada Deacon reigned. She was Labour to the bone. She told us of marches, battles and elections, and of the steady rise of the Labour Party throughout her sixty years. Ada's strong voice soared over the noise both of typewriters within and construction works outside, where a bombed church was being rebuilt.

The atmosphere was deeply political and sometimes class-conscious. My sister typists were mostly daughters of trades unionists, and anything middle class, including wine drinking and the arts, was regarded with suspicion. An exception was made for literature, and Ada often recounted the plots of the books which filled her evenings. The typing pool women were more concerned with their families, the arrival of new babies and, of course, boyfriends.

The Labour Party, Trades Union Council and Transport Workers Union shared Transport House in Smith Square. The Conservative Party offices occupied the opposite corner of the square. This was convenient all round. Smith Square was five minutes from the House of Commons and Lobby correspondents were five minutes away from many of their stories. They could move quickly between the two main political parties and some of the most important trades unionists.

In the middle of the square stood the remains of St John's, an eighteenth-century church sometimes known as

Queen Anne's Footstool. The story goes that the Queen quarrelled with Thomas Archer, the architect, kicked over a footstool and snapped, 'Well, build it like that!' as they gazed at the four legs which rose from the upturned stool. A more prosaic story is that the ground was very marshy, and the four square towers which rise from the corners of the church like legs were there to stabilise the building. They were almost all that remained of the building. The roof gaped open, and barbed wire protected the ruins from all but a congregation of pigeons. Bluebells grew around the walls in springtime; blackberries were abundant in the autumn.

Today I live just a few minutes from St John's. The political parties and trades unionists have long since left the square. I often go to concerts at the rebuilt church and look up with pride to one of the two stone pineapples above the doors. I raised the money for it when I was responsible for the Labour Party's bookshop. I levied an extra penny on each book bought, and since our books were sold at roughly wholesale price (no capitalist profit here!) no one objected.

I arrived at Transport House a year after the 1951 general election that saw the end of Clement Attlee's premiership and the return of a Conservative government and Winston Churchill. Attlee had accomplished much for the country, and his departure, unlike those of many Prime Ministers, did not end in tears. Stories of Attlee's modesty and lack of sophistication abound. Once, while in office, he was entertaining a friend in a restaurant when he realised he hadn't sufficient money with him. 'Do you think they will accept a cheque?' he was said to have asked hesitantly. On another occasion, when the press office at No. 10 wanted to install a Press Association tape machine, Attlee resisted. It was hugely expensive and, anyway, bad news travels quickly enough, he felt. But when it was explained that he could read the cricket scores at the end of each day, he agreed enthusiastically.

After a year of learning a great deal about politics from the inside, and growing used to seeing famous faces such as Guy Mollet from France and Julius Nyerere from Tanganyika waiting for the lift near the typing pool, I was promoted to the press office.

The party's press officer was Mollie Bell, a kindly, hugely experienced Scot with a handsome face. She knew every political and industrial journalist well, and many were friends. She remembered their fathers and helped their sons, and they respected and trusted her. This is gold, professionally and personally. The highest compliment one can pay a press officer is to trust them. Mollie's boss was Arthur Bax, an amiable Quaker, who was more involved in policy than with the press.

My duties were generally to make myself useful, answer

the phone, type drafts of speeches and press notices and collate copies for the press. Machines for this work were still in the future. Everyone called in to see Mollie – after all, she had the best gossip. There was often one or another young parliamentary candidate waiting in my office. I sympathised with Shirley Williams as she anticipated her first election campaign and wondered how long it would be before I was in that happy position, and I lent Barbara Castle my nail file while she waited to attend a meeting.

The air in the road outside our offices was often thick with emotion and dispute. Demonstrators, from busmen to dockers to Ford shop stewards, shouted slogans against Frank Cousins or insults at party leaders as they arrived to discuss disarmament, public ownership or the expulsion of some troublesome party member. Inside the building there was much more tolerance. We represented every shade of opinion but managed to work harmoniously together.

There was a fairly steady rhythm to our daily work in the press office, leading up to the monthly meeting of the National Executive Committee and culminating each year in our annual conference in Blackpool. Senior people stayed at the Imperial Hotel in what I then perceived as absolute luxury. The rest of us had basic accommodation in lesser hotels farther along the great promenade.

I have always loved a good speech or sermon. Our Welsh politicians combined the two, especially the great

Jim Griffiths who held packed halls spellbound with his oratory. Another whose gift for words was enhanced by his musical Welsh voice was Aneurin Bevan. In one impassioned speech which I heard, he spoke of the delusion of the television. It sounded wonderfully scornful in his Welsh accent. Bevan never used a written speech, so the journalists of his day had to rely on their verbatim shorthand. He loved hecklers. He played them like tickling a trout, teasing, agreeing and making them laugh despite their rage. I wonder if any recordings of his speeches are still in existence. Bessie Braddock was another fine orator. I saw her work on an antagonistic Labour audience at the Albert Hall until they changed their vote. Today, our orators have all gone. The last one is Betty Boothroyd. She understands the power of a beautiful voice and a warm regional accent.

Transport House in the 1950s was a mixture of the new with the very old. The lift was ancient, shaky and noisy, with unenclosed metal gates. This was an advantage in that one could see who was in the lift before making a political decision on whether to enter it. The television studio was new and well equipped. Here, we filmed and recorded inserts for party political broadcasts, and prepared new parliamentary candidates for being interviewed. There was, however, a problem with the soundproofing: the studio was next door to the ladies' cloakroom, and one of my less glamorous jobs was to make sure there were no off-stage noises during recordings.

There was an almost affectionate relationship between Labour headquarters, its members across the country and socialist parties and workers' organisations overseas. Eager young socialist politicians from across the world turned up without warning; occasionally, on Saturday mornings, I would field a future Prime Minister from East Africa or Malta, while trying to track down a senior London official to come in and meet them. Socialist mementos had been, over the years, bequeathed to the party. Portraits of pioneers were stacked in the basement to be recycled later to distant Labour halls. There was a particular huge oil painting of the leaders of the Social Democratic Federation stored in the ground-floor committee room. Its subjects included William Morris and H. M. Hyndman. At the bottom of the painting, under 'Stepping Stones to Socialism', the programme of the 1883 committee was proclaimed in letters of gold. It began with 'Nationalisation of the Land'. This was the original Labour Party programme. No self-respecting Labour MP would want this affirmation of the abandoned creed of socialism in their constituency committee room today.

I spent three happy years as maid-of-all-work in the press department, although I was no nearer Hillcroft's dream of having its own MP. I had made many friends, both straight and gay. Those worlds, alas, did not overlap in the 1950s. It is unlikely that any of my friends today would be surprised to know that I have always been gay. Almost everyone I know has friends or family who are gay; the difference now is that it is no longer an embarrassing secret.

In the cold, grey autumn of 1955, my old school friend Mary, with whom I kept in touch, rang me from Penzance, with a question that took me by surprise. 'Would you like to go to Africa?' she asked.

'You remember old Mr Richards, the jeweller?' said Mary. 'Well, his son went to the Camborne School of Mines and is now manager of a mine in Tanganyika. He wants two sensible young women to run the office, organise some entertainment at weekends, that sort of thing. The pay is very good, Bobbie, and I think we would get on, even in the bush. Could you be ready in four weeks?'

Could I? You bet I could! Mary's plan was heaven-sent. I was in trouble. At a socialist meeting, I had met a charming and very left-wing American woman who had chaired the American–Soviet Friendship Society during the war. She had a most interesting and attractive daughter, Margot, just my age and, unknown to her mother, gay. We much enjoyed each other's company and became lovers. Her mother found out and was incandescent with fury. 'I'm going to tell Hugh Gaitskell that you seduced my daughter,' she screamed.

I was terrified and embarrassed, and it wasn't even true.

On the contrary. Later, I realised that our sophisticated Labour leader would have been amused by the incident.

The following month passed in a flurry of farewells, leaving parties, inoculations against yellow fever and other diseases, and finding a trunk for all the stuff which would go by sea – including two mouth organs. I hadn't told anyone, but I loved playing the mouth organ and had a vision of sitting by a camp fire in the bush, soulfully rendering 'Clair de Lune' in the darkness.

Buying summer clothes in the late autumn was a challenge, especially as I had very little idea of what my new life would be like. I hardly knew where Tanganyika was. The mine sent us some information, mainly about health and hygiene, and I started taking anti-malaria pills. We also received an alarming book, published by the Church of Scotland, with advice on how to live in the bush. As well as recipes for cooking local foods, it included instructions on how to make soap from hippopotamus fat. I did suffer a moment of doubt at that point.

The office gave me a farewell party, and I was surprised at the warmth of the friends I had made there. I realised I would miss Transport House more than I had thought but, gratifyingly, was told that I could always return if I wanted to. I said an affectionate but not sad farewell to Margot. ('Tell your mother I have gone to Africa!') We parted as friends, and would keep in touch.

Before leaving, I went home to say farewell to my mother. She was excited for me and, as always, pleased that I was doing something different and interesting. While I was there I became aware that she was not as strong as she used to be. We went with Peggy to Truro for some last-minute shopping and Mummy found it very difficult to haul herself onto the bus. Peggy was impatient – 'Pull yourself together,' she commanded – but Mummy laughed in an embarrassed way and said that she just didn't have the strength in her legs. She also told me later that she was having very bad headaches, 'like an iron band' around her head. I urged her to go to her doctor and not just to rely on aspirin. Peggy said she would take her, so with hugs and kisses I left for London.

My bedsit in the Holloway Road went to a friend from Hillcroft. It was easy to pack up my life and fly away.

CHAPTER NINE

We took off from Blackbushe airport, a former RAF base in Hampshire, in November 1955, soon after my twenty-ninth birthday. As we boarded the plane we felt like experienced travellers. We had often gone by plane from Penzance to the Isles of Scilly and, although it was only a twenty-minute flight, it was more than most people had experienced just ten years after the war. We flew in an unpressurised Viking at only 9,000 feet all the way, so we had a wonderful view of the changing landscape below. The Alps gleamed in bright sunshine as we cruised just above them and then glided down to Nice for lunch, the first of several stops for refuelling. There were twenty-four passengers and a crew of six, and we spent the first night at the Grand Hotel Phoenicia in Valletta, its warm luxury a sharp contrast to cold, wet, battered London.

From Malta we progressed from Benina in Libya to Wadi Halfa, and then to Khartoum for an overnight stay by the Nile. Before dinner we took a taxi ride around the city and saw a fine statue of Lawrence of Arabia on a camel. Many years later I saw photographs of this statue being shipped back to the UK. Finally, we reached Nairobi and the Stanley Hotel. During the journey, I had begun learning some Swahili from the back of the Scottish manual.

'I can say elephant, lion, snake and help,' I announced proudly.

'Well, you certainly won't need snake,' said Mary. My mother never saw one in all her life.' Her mother was South African, so Mary was my authority on all things concerning the Dark Continent, and she led the way in our exploration of Kenya's capital city.

We had read of the murderous Mau Mau outrages in recent months, but we were still quite unprepared to see most of the white men and some of the women wearing guns. This did not deter Mary from hiring a car and an African driver to take us into the bush to see lion. We had an excellent and exciting introduction into the ways of the bush, and saw many lion and other big game. We questioned our driver endlessly about everything and he responded with evident pleasure in using his fluent English. Back at the hotel that evening, the other guests thought us foolhardy to have risked our lives, as they saw it.

Two days passed exploring Dar, as we in the know call it. I could hardly believe my eyes as we criss-crossed wide streets crowded with Africans and Chinese, Arabs and Indians in traditional dress, alongside Europeans from many familiar cultures. A week before I had been in the Holloway Road. This was 1955, and it was like being in a movie, especially when a tall, handsome Arab in full 'Lawrence' garb, a jewelled dagger tucked in at his waist, walked past us.

After three days we were off again, feeling like old hands as we boarded another small plane bound up-country. En route, we experienced several bumpy landings on airstrips to deposit the handful of other passengers until eventually we were the only ones left. Bernie, the pilot, had difficulty believing that we had come to work in such an isolated place, 300 miles to the next landing point – the distance from Land's End to London. As we looked down at an airstrip like a small island in an ocean of bush, Bernie announced, 'This is Mpanda.'

Down we came, and out onto the strip, our bags and baggage dumped in the dust beside us. 'Goodbye and take care,' waved Bernie, climbed back into his plane, and took off!

And there we stood, looking around at no one and nothing. Nothing, that is, but a small round hut some distance away. The silence moved in. We were in the middle of miles and miles of emptiness.

'What do we do now?' I said at last.

'Wait,' answered Mary. 'At least it's not so hot here.' Indeed, we were over 3,000 feet up, and the climate was reasonably good for most of the year.

So, wait we did – an unreal and slightly scary experience. After a while, we saw a small cloud of dust coming slowly towards us and gradually becoming a lorry. It drew to a stop, and a short nut of a man in a white shirt and long khaki shorts walked towards us.

'Good afternoon, ladies. I'm Major Gardiner, Henry Gardiner. Sorry not to have been here to greet you, but we usually wait until the plane has actually landed before coming out to the airstrip. We've had several wasted journeys when the plane hasn't turned up. Anyhow, welcome to Mpanda. We've been waiting for you for days. It's good that you've arrived on a Saturday. It will give you time to familiarise yourselves with everything before work begins. Now, which of you is which?'

He smiled warmly and shook us each by the hand before loading us and our belongings into his lorry and off we went on the first of our countless bumpy journeys along a rough road in Tanganyika. On the way, the major kept up a running commentary on what we were seeing and where we were going.

We passed the main mine office where we would be working alongside Major Gardiner, who was the chief administrator for the mining company. It was beside a large lake. 'We built that,' said Henry Gardiner, with pride. 'We diverted the water from Lake Tanganyika. You need plenty of water on a mine.' We passed the Mpanda Club. 'We'll take you tomorrow; we always have drinks there on Sunday mornings before lunch. It's a tradition.' The residential quarters were, he explained, on the side of the hill, the houses far apart. 'After all, we have the whole of Africa.'

Arriving at a big, brick-built bungalow with a wide veranda and large, flowering shrubs all around it, the major drew to a stop. 'This is your house, ladies. I will introduce you to your boys. I assume you haven't had house servants before?' He didn't need an answer. 'You have five here: a cook and his assistant, a houseboy and his assistant, and a garden boy. They understand English, but I hope you will soon learn some Swahili. I have agreed their wages, so don't give them any more. That only upsets arrangements for everyone else.'

Major Gardiner had explained on the way that he'd come on from India with his wife, Jean. After independence they'd decided to leave, but they had loved their colonial life and couldn't bear the thought of living in the UK with its bad weather and socialism. Africa had been the solution. 'It will see us out until retirement.'

'What will you do then?'

'South Africa, of course. Cape Town.' I have often wondered how the Gardiners would have fared when that beautiful country lost its white masters.

The staff had lined up to greet us: young, smiling, black faces; slim bodies clad in white vests and khaki shorts.

'They will do everything for you, young ladies. Cook your meals, wash and iron your clothes and keep the bungalow clean,' said the major, effecting the staff's introduction to us. 'It is particularly important that they – and you – keep the inner doors and windows shut and that they spray all of the rooms, morning and night. We don't want you going down with malaria – or anything else for that matter.'

On that note, promising to collect us at six o'clock for a small dinner party his wife had arranged at their house, he left, roaring off in a cloud of dust.

Our bungalow was cool and spacious: perfect for parties, we thought. At one end were two large bedrooms, separated by a very large bathroom and, at the other, a kitchen and storeroom. In between was a vast living room with an immense fireplace – the only one in Mpanda, as we learnt. We unpacked the essentials we had brought to tide us over till the arrival of our main luggage from its long sea voyage.

'I don't like the thought of them washing all our clothes,' said Mary in an unnecessary whisper. 'Not all of them.'

'I expect they're used to it, but we'll ask Mrs Gardiner tonight.'

Dinner was elegantly served and delicious. We began with tilapia, a fish from the lake, followed by beautifully tender venison which, as Jean Gardiner explained, was shot at weekends by engineers who hunted. There was no shortage of game but, as she told us, beef was a different matter. 'It has to walk 300 miles from Northern Rhodesia. We tenderise all the meat here with pawpaw leaves. Three days in the fridge and it's fine.'

The other guests that evening were Paolo Cigaleone, a senior mining engineer, his wife Lucia, and two English senior mining engineers. They were all very friendly and answered our questions in detail. We learnt that there were only four wives on the mine, and now we had already met two of them. Most of the engineers were either bachelors or had left their families at home – which might be Italy, France, Austria, Canada, the USA, Australia, South Africa and, of course, Cornwall.

'We are a miniature League of Nations,' smiled Jean, 'though we get on with each other rather better.' She was wearing a low-cut sleeveless cotton dress, her make-up was understated, and her skin deeply tanned. Paolo Cigaleone was, of course, Italian, and was the deputy to our boss, William Richards. Paolo was a jolly man who loved good food. His wife cooked delectable Italian meals, which we were occasionally invited to share, and she also taught me a little Italian.

Henry Gardiner – we were all on first-name terms now – drove us back in the lorry. 'We are delighted that you're here,' he said with a huge smile. 'We were not at all sure what to expect. This is an experiment for us, you see. We usually employ male clerks because it's quite a tough life, but you two will do admirably.'

That was a really nice note on which to end our first evening, which had been a very pleasant introduction to this new life we were entering. And we'd learnt some interesting facts about the people there. Apart from the professional engineers from the four corners of the world, the European miners were Italians from Bergamo, who were housed in a camp of their own. Mary and I never went there, but we would soon sometimes hear them at night, singing operatic choruses as they returned from ... somewhere... The African miners, though, were in the majority. The tribal chiefs were paid a fixed amount of cash per head to send us their best men. They, too, lived in a separate camp and, as we came to know, they also sang at night – often haunting African songs, quite new to us. The social life of the mine centred on the club, which was for Europeans only, and this was where we were being taken the next morning at eleven.

I thought sleep would be difficult. Everything was so new and so different, not least negotiating our mosquito nets, tucking them in all around the bed then crawling underneath and tucking the last bit of netting into the mattress.

After satisfyingly hot, albeit rather brownish-coloured, baths, we enjoyed a perfectly cooked English breakfast, but one that began with sugar-sweet, lightly chilled pawpaw dressed with the juice of fresh lime. Coming from 1950s London and post-war food rationing, this was a novelty indeed, and one to which I became easily accustomed. The sun shone on a hot summer's day, we wore our prettiest cotton dresses and sandals, and speculated, somewhat apprehensively, about the men who would, we hoped, be our friends for the next three years.

'I wonder what they'll think of us,' Mary said. I had no doubt about what they would think of Mary. She was very tall, slim and very good-looking, with shoulder-length black hair and dark eyes. I was five foot three, my brown hair short and curly and, at nine stone, rather well covered!

When Henry Gardiner proudly ushered us into the club and down the steps leading to a long bar, our entrance was met by a sea of upturned faces and then what seemed to us to be a rather disconcerting ripple of amusement. We were greeted by the men we had met the night before and, once supplied with large gins, enjoyed meeting some of our immediate neighbours.

'Why were you so amused to see us?' I asked one of them. He looked embarrassed. 'Come on! Tell me!'

'Well, we had a sort of bet about what you would look like, and someone predicted that one of you would be tall and thin and the other short and fat. Of course, you're not a bit like that really,' he added hastily.

I immediately resolved to give up cooked breakfasts.

The African barman wore a long white shirt, called a *kanzu*, and a red fez. He knew everyone's name and what they liked to drink. As a Muslim, he was forbidden to drink alcohol.

'But aren't they tempted?' I asked my new friend, Jack Carlyon.

'Their religion is very strong, much stronger than ours. Nothing would make him touch a drop. That's why they make such good barmen.'

We noticed the whisky drinkers filling their glasses to the brim with water, unlike London men who added just a splash. It seemed soft and unmanly somehow, but when we learnt how much the miners sweated underground – and how much they drank – we changed our opinion about what was 'unmanly'.

We were introduced to many convivial men that first club Sunday morning and promptly forgot most of their names, but we certainly remembered two monks in white robes.

'Priests, White Fathers, they're called,' Stanley, a senior mining engineer explained. 'They come here for ten years at a time to look after their flocks.' He smiled ironically. 'When East Africa was divided up into separate countries, the churches involved themselves, too. Kenya, for example, is strongly Church of Scotland, but here you're in a Catholic area. You'll see the White Fathers on Sundays chasing the Italians to get them to Mass. They are excellent company actually, very well educated, and they play a good game of bridge.'

Gradually the men left for lunch, coming to say goodbye to us before revving their lorries in farewell. We returned to our new home with Henry, who checked to see that our 'boys' were looking after us properly and that the traditional Sunday curry was ready.

'You'll find transport very easy,' he told us before leaving. 'One or other of us will always be ready to take you to the club or the *dukas*.' The *dukas* were the Indian stores that sold all the basics from rice to gin. They were simple structures, with a musty dry smell that made me feel they hadn't changed much since Livingstone passed through on his way to the lake. Nearby, a series of big rondavels – round, thatched roof structures that mimicked the design of African tribal huts – housed the Mpanda Hotel. This was where one went for dinner to have a change from the club. That, in essence, was our community. There was one telephone on the mine and one plane a week.

We spent that first Sunday afternoon writing letters home. We knew that some of what we described would shock our friends but, on the other hand, my parents would be delighted to learn of our colonial luxury. As we gradually grew to know our new friends, we realised that it would not be sensible to discuss politics. Already Andy, a mining engineer, had teased me about 'your' dreadful socialist government, and I had to point out to him that the government was, in fact, Conservative. That Conservative policies struck them as being socialist only confirmed most of the engineers in their resolve to stay away from the UK and end their days in South Africa!

On Monday morning, Henry Gardiner turned up promptly at 7.30 a.m. to take us to our first day in the office. We worked 8 a.m.–12 p.m. and 4-6 p.m. Apart from the business of the mine, we were also a branch of East African Airways, and had to issue tickets and deal with cargo. It made sense, as all the passengers were mine staff, apart from one or two hopeful geologists.

Later that morning we had our first meeting with our boss, William Richards, the mine manager. We talked about Penzance, and then Mr Richards said, 'You must be weighed. We'll check your weight every few months – can't have you getting ill.'

Neither of us was particularly thrilled about this, especially when we were taken to a big shed where several miners were weighing ore. Here we were lifted on to huge scales before a respectful audience, and Henry Gardiner entered our weight in a register.

'I feel like the Aga Khan,' said Mary after the weighing, 'but no rubies.'

CHAPTER TEN

It did not take us long to get used to our new life. We were young, eager for adventure and resilient. It was sheer heaven to have our housework and cooking done for us, and to be in such solicitous company. The men admired us for having the spirit to work so far away from home, and always seemed delighted to drive us anywhere we needed to go. We were expected to work hard, but we found the work easy. I didn't mind going back to secretarial work, since it was giving me an extraordinary adventure and great experiences to store for the future. We came to love our bungalow, surrounded with glorious pink and purple bougainvillea, and where everything indoors was on a luxuriously large scale.

Every day we learnt about something new. Our dining chairs, which were almost too heavy to lift, were made of

African teak, a good, hard wood for carving, and you could find lovely carved African heads on sale at the *dukas*. Our 'boys' lived in small shacks at the back of the garden, and we learnt that the cook, as the senior member of the staff, had his wife living with him. We learnt about the climate. We had arrived near the end of the dry season, and out in the bush the grass was shoulder high, the weather hot and dry, and we could feel (or felt we could feel) the thirsty land's longing for water.

One evening, Mary went to her bedroom and I went for a shower, where I found a large hose pipe neatly coiled on the bathroom floor.

'Mary,' I called out, 'why do you think someone has left a hose pipe in the bathroom?'

'I don't know. Something to do with the plumbing, I suppose.'

I went to take a closer look. The hose gradually began to uncoil.

'Mary! It's a snake!'

'Don't be ridiculous.' But she opened her door, took one look and screaming 'Oh my God!', slammed the door shut.

I ran into the living room, shouting '*Nyoka mkubwa! Upasi sana!*' (Large snake! Come quickly!). The servants came running. '*Wapi memsahib?*' I pointed to the bathroom. They searched, but it had gone. The following day, we learnt what you should do when you see a snake. You certainly do not slam the door and run away: you watch it, our friend Jack Carlyon told us. WATCH IT?!

'Yes. To see where it goes. It is fairly unlikely to attack you, especially a spitting cobra, which is what yours was. Your bungalow has been empty for some time and the bathroom floor would have been nice and cool in this hot weather.'

We were both frightened, and it took us a while to use the bathroom again without a cautious search of all the corners, but we enjoyed telling our story to our new friends and in letters home.

One evening we were greeted by our staff, lined up on the veranda steps as we returned home from work. The head boy held up a very long, dead snake.

'*Nyoka, memsahib*. We have caught him.' We were surprised and horrified – and relieved. We congratulated them, and Jack, who had driven us home, said we should give them a tip. We gave them ten shillings, about a quarter of the cook's weekly pay.

'Where did you find it?' Jack asked.

'Under the mattress on Memsahib Mary's bed.'

'Oh my God! I won't be able to sleep there ever again.'

'Of course you will. It's dead now, it won't be back,' Jack consoled.

I was brisker. 'At least it shows how thorough the boys are. Shall we take some photographs?'

I held the snake by its tail, my hand stretched high above my head. It was very heavy. Mary stood with the cook, who held it for her. I asked Jack what would happen to it now.

'They'll probably eat it and sell the skin to the Italians. The Italians are great craftsmen. They will turn the skin into beautiful, soft leather.'

Later that night Mary was still reluctant to go to bed, despite having downed nearly a tumbler-full of whisky. 'How do you know that it doesn't have a mate?'

'They never do,' I said. 'They live alone and only copulate once in their lives. I found a book about them and read it before we left London.'

It was a total fabrication but it worked; and so did the whisky. Mary slept well. It was I who didn't.

*   *   *

We quickly adjusted to the routine of the mining community. The engineers were eager to tell us how the mine worked, and we learnt how the ore was crushed and of the various chemical washes which were used to extract gold, copper, silver and lead from the rock. Mr Richards was pleased that his plan was working. It was he who had persuaded the board in Belgium to make the unconventional decision to employ women instead of men at the office. It makes for a more civilised life, he explained to us. So with four wives, a nurse, Mary and me, we were an outpost of feminine civilisation in this remote corner of Africa.

The local tribe led a simple pastoral life. Mary and I were very conscious that Livingstone and Stanley had explored this area and we were only forty miles from Ujiji on Lake Tanganyika, where they had had their momentous meeting. We discussed the changes which the mine had brought to the Africans in Mpanda and decided that it was probably true that their lives had been improved. They were intelligent and quickly learnt to use the mining equipment and to drive the huge lorries with their many gears. We also soon became aware that the Europeans deeply believed in their superiority and their right to rule. At first we tried to have serious discussions with others about this, but we failed to achieve any recognition that the future might be different. So we decided to talk about giraffe and the various types of antelope, and avoid arguments where we could.

Wednesdays and Saturdays were film nights, which were always held in the open air, and watched with a litre bottle of beer to hand. We wore long sleeves, long trousers and covered any exposed areas with Dimp to keep the mosquitos away. We took our anti-malaria pills every day. At 3,000 feet we were up above the tsetse flies, but we knew that any bite could fester, so we were careful. Club members took turns in choosing the programme, a democratic process that resulted, on one memorable occasion, in a young Italian miner choosing ten Esther Williams films. We all became expert critics of her spectacular swimming and stylish swimsuits, and by the end of the month we decided that she was rather a good actress, too.

In our contracts with the mine, Mary and I had agreed to take charge of organising entertainments. We celebrated everything we could think of, from the Queen's birthday to the feast of Corpus Christi. The latter was the Penzance feast, celebrated every year since very ancient times. I sent stories and photographs of these activities back to my old editor – dating from the Isles of Scilly days – of *The Cornishman*. Mary was none too pleased when she received letters commenting, somewhat unkindly, on her achievement in coming third in the egg-and-spoon race.

We did everything on a big scale at the mine. After all, as Henry had remarked, we had the whole of Africa at our disposal. Thus, for Guy Fawkes Day, the engineers built a truly huge fire and an equally huge effigy. It was about eight feet tall, with eyes made of half a ping-pong ball and tiny light bulbs behind them attached to a battery. When the Guy was put on the massive – now lit – fire, those eyes glared at us, and as the flames took hold they flashed intermittently and eerily. We all felt a bit uncomfortable. 'Too realistic, perhaps?' Jack Carlyon murmured. The Africans watched and wondered at this spectacle from a distance.

We held lorry races on the airstrip. These were illegal, so we didn't publicise them. I had acquired my own vehicle: a Hudson Terraplane. An ex-field ambulance, it resembled a tank rather than a car, but I bought it quite cheaply and, like the men with their lorries, I had free petrol from the mine. It was a monster with huge wheels and I loved it. It was odd how things just turned up on the mine, left there by some miner going home perhaps, or sometimes a geologist passing through on his way to even remoter areas. I practised driving it on the airstrip, with advice from Stanley. I drove Mary to the office every day, to the club in the evenings and to the *dukas* for our shopping. We were glad to be independent.

I also acquired a .22 rifle and discovered, to my surprise, that I had good hand–eye co-ordination. I've always been short-sighted so it was thrilling when Jack told me that, if I practised, I might make quite a good shot. After the Sheffield peace camp I had vowed never to go camping again, but I was reassured that this would be different and much more comfortable; besides, you will never see any game if you don't wake up in the bush.

Our guns were carried by tribesmen chosen for their hunting skills. We drove out into the bush in the early morning, before the day grew hot. When we reached a likely spot, we followed our guides through the shoulder-high grass as quietly as we could. They could see animals through the thickest trees, but it took us many months before we could spot anything unless it moved. Sometimes we passed a giraffe, gazing down at us, quite unafraid, and watched herds of antelope, leaping like ballet dancers as they ran away. When I was allowed to, I shot small creatures like guinea fowl. We ate what we shot, and while I had no difficulty in justifying this killing to myself, I was uncomfortable about big game. A couple of the miners had licences to shoot four elephants a year, and they sold the tusks for quite large sums. The Africans loved going on these shoots, as they could cut off all the elephant hair; this they made into bracelets, which they believed gave them great power and which they sold for good money.

As we adapted to our environment, we also grew accustomed to our domestic wildlife. We liked the geckos, the little lizards which darted up the walls. We remained perfectly calm when a mother iguana with four babies appeared on our roof gutter. We had been wondering for weeks what was making such a heavy, dragging noise above us and here was the culprit. There were no more snakes in the house, though I did share the backseat of Jack Carlyon's jeep with a stunned puff adder. We saw it on the road one moonlit night when he was driving me home from the club. Jack hit it on the head with a spanner and threw it into the back of the jeep. He then put me in the back, handed me the spanner and told me to hit it again if it moved. I watched it like a hawk and could see its body rippling under its skin, a weird sight, but it stayed still.

Occasionally, we held our own dinner parties on a Saturday evening, which pleased our cook who devised great menus to show off his skill. We invited six of the mining engineers at a time and our well-trained servants did all the work. All we had to do was to decide on the drinks; a simple task: a crate of beer or a bottle of whisky per guest and plenty of bottled water. It sounds more than excessive to write this today, but no one seemed to get drunk. A huge amount of water was consumed and our guests always drove home without mishap.

Halfway through our contract, we were entitled to two weeks' leave. Mary went first and chose to visit cousins in South Africa. It was while she was away that I received a letter from Geoff telling me that my mother had died from an inoperable brain tumour. She was in hospital for only a short time, and Peggy had insisted that she should be moved from the general ward into a private room. I grieved deeply for my mother, whose life had been cut short at the age of fifty-seven, just when things were becoming so much easier for her. I also grieved for myself that I would never now have the opportunity to give her some of the luxuries she had never had, or take her to London, to the concerts and theatres that she would have so loved. I was comforted by Geoff's thanks to me for a long, loving letter

I had written to her a month before, when I had told her to brush up her French because I was going to take her to Paris as soon as I returned. My father's attendance at the funeral was the last time he ever came home.

Mary was a great comfort when she returned from Johannesburg, and we agreed that families were sometimes difficult to cope with.

For my leave I chose Zanzibar. I saw the old slave market and, when I was peering through the ornate gates of a mosque, I was invited in and proudly given a private tour. It had been built for the Aga Khan, and there was a luxurious bedroom where the huge bed was made up with silk sheets, covered in fresh rose petals – changed every day in readiness for him whenever he might arrive. I also saw the sultan in a red car. All around me the local people fell to their knees as he passed by. I bought a heavy silver bracelet which was weighed to determine its price. Once again, I felt as if I was in an early film as I watched some impossibly grand dhow captains go by, ornate daggers at their waists.

When I returned to the mine, I suggested to Mary that we should organise a Cornish picnic. We showed our cook how to make pasties and saffron cake, and I arranged to have Cornish clotted cream flown out from Truro. We held our picnic on the airstrip. There were fifteen of us, and the group photograph of Mr Richards and his compatriots eating pasties duly appeared in *The Cornishman*. The local paper at home was the main outlet for my journalistic ambitions, but sometimes a story merited space and a picture in the Dar es Salaam *Standard*.

My biggest story was when our cook told me of the death of a black man, 'a great man, *bwana mkubwa*', he said. I decided to look into this, and discovered that an old man, revered by all, who lived near the lake, had recently died and that thousands would attend his funeral. No one really knew how old he was, but he was generally thought to be over eighty – a great age in that part of the world. Apparently, when he was a boy, he was caught by slavers, but rescued by a missionary who bought him for a bar of soap and educated him. He, in turn, became a missionary himself. That story was used not only in East Africa, but by Reuters too.

In the office, Mary typed the important documents about shipments of lead, copper, silver and gold, and helped to organise the lorries and drivers who would make the 500-mile journey to Ndola, in what is now Zambia. I typed correspondence with Tabora and Dodoma, the regional administrative centres for Tanganyika, and looked after the East African Airways business. There were a few challenging moments. For example, when the mine dam burst and we had to walk along a plank over a raging torrent to reach our office. 'Keep your eyes on me,' Stanley shouted from the office side. 'One step at a time, slowly, and don't look down,' and we crossed in safety. This went on for four days.

We were both excited when Mr Ionides, of whom we had heard much talk at the club, turned up at the office. A loner who lived in the bush and caught snakes for a living, he was considered something of a hero because of the dangers of the bush, not to mention the snakes. Now he was in our office: a deeply tanned, wiry little man, accompanied by a large wooden crate.

'Air freight,' he said. 'For Nairobi and on to London.'

'What's in the crate?' I asked, not really wanting to know.

'Snakes,' he replied. 'Wild snakes. They can't get out and, in any case, they're sleeping. I have given them a good dinner.'

I looked up the regulations for transporting live snakes and found the right forms. After Mr Ionides left, Mary and I, slightly nervous, had a good look at the crate. It seemed quiet. Our weekly flight was on Saturdays, two days away, and we didn't completely relax until we had driven to the airstrip with Mr Ionides and supervised the loading and departure of his crate. The pilot was not at all worried about his cargo and had clearly met similar passengers before.

One Sunday, we were at home tucking into the traditional East African lunch of chicken curry, accompanied by several side dishes of tomatoes, nuts, cucumber and whatever else was available, when we noticed that some little bits of plaster were falling off the wall. Gradually, the room began to shake, and we heard our houseboys shouting out from the garden for us to join them.

'I think this is an earthquake, Mary,' I said, but Mary disagreed. 'It's just a tremor; they often have them in South Africa. The boys are overreacting.'

We went on with our lunch, and observed a split opening down the wall. I felt a strange sensation, rather like standing on a platform on the Underground in London when another train is passing underneath.

I didn't want to appear frightened, but I was. Very. If this was a tremor, I would have hated to experience something worse. 'Are you sure about this, Mary? Your face is quite white.'

'You should see yours!' she replied, and we both decided to move. Before we could stand up there was a great screaming of brakes and Stanley rushed in, out of breath and anxious. 'Are you all right?'

We reassured him that we were, and I remarked that it was quite a violent tremor... wasn't it?

'Violent tremor?' exclaimed Stanley. 'It was a bloody great earthquake! Force eight on the Richter scale. There's one dead and several hurt at the *dukas*, and you just went on with your lunch!'

He stared at us in a mixture of shock and admiration. We had already acquired a reputation for being two unusually intrepid young women. Tanganyika was a huge country with a very small white population and gossip went from airstrip to airstrip. We were just being British, we said, as we shook the plaster from our hair.

*   *   *

Clearly, it would have been unlikely for two young, unattached women to live in the remote bush for three years with some thirty virile mining engineers without some flirtation and sex. The men were tanned and fit – they had to be to climb the vertical ladders underground. In the 1950s, contraception was not that easy to buy in the wilds of East Africa, hundreds of miles from the nearest pharmacy. We could hardly ask the mine doctor for advice as he was a Polish Catholic, so the mine nurse was our only hope. Flora McGregor was a middle-aged Scot who had come to East Africa soon after gaining her qualifications. She had worked for years in Nairobi and Dar before joining the company for a quieter life. She was unattached and rarely joined in our social activities.

We invited Flora to supper and asked her advice. Mary, of course, didn't know that I was hardly likely to need it – or so I thought, but some of the men were very attractive and three years is a long time. We waited anxiously for her advice. 'Well,' she said, 'if I were you I would be very careful.'

And so we were.

*   *   *

Some things cannot be anticipated, and it came as a sharp blow when Mary became ill. The mine doctor diagnosed a return of the TB she had suffered when she was seventeen. We didn't really believe him, but Mary was certainly very poorly and we decided that she should return home. I was asked if I would like to leave as well. Could I bear to live here on my own? I thought I could, and decided to stay. I was given a smaller house, closer to neighbours, and with tears and kisses we waved Mary off to London. It was over a year before I saw her again. She was perfectly well and looked like a model. She had a good job as a director's PA at a pharmaceutical company, and lived in a roomy flat in Ealing. She also had a boyfriend with a string of degrees who taught at a college in Hertfordshire and had a passion for classical music.

I missed Mary very much in Mpanda, but the work kept me busy. The company advertised for a secretary to join me, but when a young woman with excellent qualifications arrived at the airstrip, she caused utter consternation. She was mixed race and the mine managers were firm: she couldn't stay. She should have told us, they complained – it just will not do. We can't have her in the club.

I was furious. She seemed very nice and she could live with me, I told them. I expressed myself frankly, making no secret of my shock, but to no avail. 'You don't under-stand. You haven't lived here,' they said, and despite my protestations, she was sent back to Nairobi and I worked on alone.

The final year of my contract soon passed, and when the time came for my departure, the engineers were very sorry to see me go – they had already heard the bad news that I was to be replaced by two young men. The company had searched in vain for two more young women to come to the mine, but it seemed that in neither Cornwall nor London were there two adventurous young women willing to succeed us.

Although, of course, I was sad to say goodbye to the men, I was by this time longing to return to the UK. I hadn't seen the sea – other than a brief glimpse in Zan-zibar – for more than three years, and I wanted to walk on Cornish cliffs and watch the waves crashing against the rocks. I was also missing the bustle and sophistica-tion of London: concerts and theatres, buses and taxis – and girls.

I was asked if there was anything special which I would like as a farewell present. I had already, regretfully, had to return a dear little handgun – 'it would fit into your hand-bag, Bobbie' – but I had no difficulty in deciding on my special present. We had seen dozens of films set in Africa, in which elegantly dressed film stars camped deep in the bush, their make-up perfect and not a hair out of place as they sipped cocktails served by uniformed waiters. That was what I wanted.

And that was what I got, a memorable day. It was kept secret until the last minute; I was simply told to wear my best dress as I was to meet someone important. I wondered if, perhaps, the governor was to visit. He loved making the long journey to see us, but he hadn't been for nearly a year.

I was driven many miles through the tall grass into a clearing in the bush. There, covered with a white cloth and laid for lunch, was a long table and the club staff alongside in their white kanzus and red fezzes, bobbing in greeting and wreathed in smiles. I had my film-star moment and if I didn't look like a star, I certainly felt like one.

I gave each of my servants a month's wages and the cook my radio so that he could listen to the football from Dar on Saturdays. I was touched that they seemed truly sorry I was leaving.

I returned to London in October 1957, in time for my thirty-first birthday in November. The journey, in a Comet jet that left from Nairobi, was rather faster than the six days it had taken on our outward flight. This time we flew at 30,000 feet, and there was no chance of seeing herds of game below.

My three years away had seen me face some loneliness, real dangers and some unusual responsibilities. And I had turned down an offer of marriage. My heterosexual inter-lude had been lovely but it could not last, and marriage would have been deeply unfair to a very nice man. I knew my nature. I might well have been more attracted to my bridesmaid than to my groom!

In short, I had grown up.

CHAPTER ELEVEN

I had two goals on my return to London: to resume my happy social life among friends with whom I had no need to dissemble, and to find an interesting job where I could write. The first of my friends to respond to the telephone calls from my hotel room was Chris Athey, the woman who had lured me away from the Odeon house magazine to further education at Hillcroft. She was no longer the late-night club-goer I remembered, but had become a respected academic – an authority on pre-school cognitive development, and was writing a book on the subject.

Chris's seriousness and her achievements much impressed me, but I wanted to play. I wanted to hear the gossip about the Gateways where we had spent so many happy evenings, but she wanted to tell me about the sand and water tray! We had always had two lives, our evening lives in raffish clubs where our friends included ex-prisoners and prostitutes, and our respectable daytime careers. Now Chris had given up the nightlife. One reason for this soon became clear: a spectacularly good-looking BBC journalist, Meryl O'Keeffe, with whom she was becoming much occupied. The other reason was the increasing demands of her research.

So I went to the Gateways on my own. It was not a happy evening. There was no one there I knew and no one seemed to remember me. I hadn't thought that three years would make such a difference; it certainly hadn't in Penzance. I asked after Jeanette, the cheeky Yorkshire girl I had so often danced with. The woman behind the bar told me that she had been murdered, and reminded me how she was always taking risks. We had all told her not to go with dodgy men from those pubs around King's Cross, but she wouldn't listen. I remembered the black eye and cut lip: 'all part of the game', she had laughed, when I questioned her.

I left the club early and wondered if I, too, was perhaps growing away from my former life.

While Chris was clearly no help with my social life, she proved heaven-sent when she asked if I would like to share a large flat in Finchley Road. It was big enough for three, and the third flatmate would be Stella Tanner, one of the Tanner Sisters, a famous singing double act. I happily exchanged a lonely hotel room for a home, but my hoard of money was steadily decreasing. The cost of living in London was immense after Mpanda, and I needed a job. This was in 1958; I was thirty-two years old, and it was time to stop playing. I had no useful publishing or journalism contacts and my CV was anything but straightforward.

I tried in vain to convince publishers and newspaper editors that I was a highly efficient secretary, and that I would be willing to start at the bottom and work my way up. I felt hugely frustrated by this apparently insurmountable wall. I thought I had a good record, if patchy. My first poem was published when I was ten, my first broadcast made when I was sixteen. I had been assistant editor of a magazine and had written a regular column in *The Cornishman* for three years. Alas, I was the only person impressed with my achievements. There were, of course, the interruptions when I dived in and out of typing pools, went to Hillcroft and worked on a mine in Africa. But still…

Really unhappy and depressed, I had lunch with a friend from the Labour Party who suggested I should come back to Transport House. 'It's an exciting time now, lots going on and there's going to be an election soon,' she enthused. I wrote to Morgan Phillips, who remembered me, and offered me a job as assistant to Mollie Bell, the chief press officer. I was thrilled at being given a lifeline. The salary was very modest, but certainly enough to live on and pay my share of the Finchley Road flat.

Chris, Stella and I were harmonious flatmates. We

gathered in the kitchen in the evenings, when Chris would tell us about her pre-school research project. She had a control group of Asian families, and was indignant that when doing her tests on the infants the mothers wanted to join in. Even the fathers, sometimes, she complained. I wondered if she shouldn't be writing about these Asian families who clearly longed for education instead of about infant cognition, but she felt that I was not taking her research seriously enough.

I would talk about the day's happenings at Transport House. We were all three backsliding members of the Labour Party, but as the election approached we became more partisan. Sometimes I was able to explain the story behind a headline or relay some tale of the iniquities of the Tory press.

Stella was the star in all senses. She sometimes burst into the kitchen late in the evening, bringing the excitement of show business, the theatre and whom she had met that evening. We never needed to go to a musical while living with Stella. She came back from first nights and acted the whole show for us, every part, and kept us enthralled while we plied her with coffee.

My desire to visit Cornwall was no longer the same as it had been before my mother died. My father had never returned home after joining the army, where he retrained after the war as a factory technician. He found comfortable lodgings with a widow in Stroud and, in time, I went to see him there and found, as I had expected, that he was now living happily with his landlady. I tried not to be judgemental, but my loyalty remained wholly with my mother and it wasn't easy to share meals with Daddy as part of a couple, especially when they told me that they had been on holiday to Paris.

Transport House had also changed in my absence – in this case for the better. There was a new energy throughout the building, and now that I was no longer in the typing pool I was treated differently. Mollie Bell became more of a friend than a boss and I was included in conversations with senior people. I almost hadn't lasted the first week, however, after the *Daily Express* rang within a couple of days. 'You're the new girl ... nice to meet you ... I wonder if you can help me, I've misplaced Tom Driberg's phone number ... do you have it there by any chance...?' Eager to be helpful, I found the number in a file of MPs' details and gave it to him.

I had never heard of ex-directory and I certainly had not heard of Driberg's notorious sexual activities. There was an immediate complaint from him. The *Express* was never going to print anything favourable; why had I done it? Mollie Bell forgave me, and I soon learnt some of the wicked ways of our great British press. I decided that politicians were like actors. They needed publicity but they were wary of it too; they were performers, professionals. Most of them spent hours drafting and redrafting their speeches, but a few – notably Aneurin Bevan – spoke without notes. Mollie herself was good with words and had once written a romantic novel. It was published, and the proceeds paid for her first visit to Paris. Arthur Bax, our boss, was trusted by all the party leaders, however much they distrusted each other.

I was now an eager convert to the Labour Party. My Cornish liberalism had easily moved a little to the left, and I soon believed in socialist principles as completely as I had once believed in the Creed. I watched the women candidates as they hurried in to see Arthur or Mollie. They were all cradle socialists and clearly on their way to powerful political careers. In Mollie's office I met women such as Betty Boothroyd, Jo Richardson, Gwyneth Dunwoody and Shirley Williams – who greeted Mollie with a kiss. 'Am I going to win?' she asked, her blue eyes shining with excitement. Like almost all the women, she had to fight several elections and by-elections before she eventually did win. I was not used to meeting strong career women who had the confidence to stand up in public, and wondered whether I might ever even dare to aspire to a political career.

The two most important dates for any political party are the annual conference and the general election. The conferences are usually held in September before the House reassembles after the long summer break – a break originally put in place so that MPs could go back to their acres and help with the harvest. The Labour Party held their conference in Blackpool. The popular seaside towns I knew were Cornish, very quiet and genteel places like Newquay, and I was unprepared for the brash atmosphere of this northern holiday resort. It was triumphantly working class, like the party itself, I thought.

Much of our time at the conference was spent churning out copies of speeches for the journalists who thronged our office. Sometimes I staggered off to the press room with armfuls of releases literally hot off the machine. I loved the press room. It was exciting to see and hear journalists from all over the world, beating up their typewriters or dictating their copy down the phones. The noise was deafening, the air blue with cigarette smoke and the room rocked with energy. Piles of dirty teacups and overflowing ashtrays were evidence of their hard work.

All party conferences were hectically social. Lunches, receptions, drinks and formal dinners were given by the press, regional political groups, the BBC and, later, ITV companies. Several years on, I hosted parties myself at these conferences. They are highly charged events where political reputations can be made or ruined in moments. At Labour conferences there were also parties given by the trades unions, and that first year I was invited to the Boiler-makers' party, where the decision on what to drink was made very easy: the choice was beer or whisky – just like the mining engineers, I mused. There was a tall, pink-faced woman in spectacles present, who seemed very popular.

Mollie told me she was Anne Godwin, the only woman trades union leader. She ran the Clerical Workers Union – my union, Mollie pointed out. She was really powerful, much more so than a backbench MP. I watched her sipping whisky and holding court, and wondered if I should perhaps turn my ambitions in that direction.

When there was a lull in our work, I was able to go into the conference hall. Sometimes I was lucky and heard a major speech, but often there were boring stretches when motions were amended or a card vote taken. In the 1950s, a card vote took up a great deal of time as every card had to be counted. Some were for one vote, but in the case of the unions a card might represent many thousands of votes all counted by hand. When the time came for the leader's speech, the high point of the week, we all assembled. Before the 1959 election there were impassioned speeches as the left and right wings of the party struggled to win crucial votes. I heard Aneurin Bevan – who had famously declared in 1957 that he did not wish to be sent naked into the council chambers of Europe – in the debate on nuclear weapons. And I heard Hugh Gaitskell make his fight, fight and fight again speech, a truly passionate cry at the height of the nuclear disarmament debate. It was years before I realised how courageous he had been. In those days I was seduced by the simplicities of the left and I was slow to grow up politically.

A unique tradition at Labour Party conferences was the closing speech on behalf of the press. One of the most memorable of these was when Michael Stewart of *The Guardian* contrasted the 'rich red wine of socialism with the cocoa of conformity'. Sadly, he was unable to enjoy the congratulations of senior party members as he suffered a fatal heart attack immediately after leaving the platform. It was a great end, though, for a much-loved journalist.

I loved the theatre of politics, the excitement of debate and the results of the votes. The general election was only months away and the old war horses at Transport House were, after two election defeats, daring to hope once more. The young ones were sure we would win. Trade at the Marquis of Granby across the road was very brisk; journalists and party workers moved to and fro between the Houses of Parliament and Smith Square to call on us and on Conservative Central Office in the neighbouring corner. Morgan Phillips began holding daily press conferences and won respect and admiration with his frank answers to questions. Instead of making political jibes at the opposition, he explained policies by giving background facts and statistics. Conservative Central Office finally had to reply, and Lord Hailsham presided over their press conferences. Reports and rebuttals were hurled across the square, chased by the hungry journalists. After the last press conference at Transport House, all of them, whatever their paper's allegiance, stood and applauded Morgan.

Next day, 8 October 1959, all the complicated apparatus for recording election results had been installed. A huge board listed every constituency and special lighting for television and state-of-the-art microphones were installed. But by the end of the day no one had bothered to complete the board: as the results had come in, it was clear that the Tories had won for a third time. When I walked out into the square past the loudspeaker vans, Central Office was ablaze with lights. Behind me, our lights were already going out. I learnt the next day that a turnout of nearly 80 per cent had brought a Tory majority of 100.

The following morning I went into the office early. Mollie was red-eyed and quiet, the general mood funereal, as we awaited the arrival of our defeated leader, Hugh Gaitskell. We lined the steps and cheered Gaitskell into the building. Perhaps it was the applause, or perhaps it was the gallant smile on his face, but my mood lightened and I knew what I was going to do.

Life at the mine had made me strong and self-reliant. I felt sure I could cope with misogynistic politicians and, indeed, with the snakes that one finds hidden in all political parties.

PART III

SNAKES
AND
LADDERS

CHAPTER TWELVE

I was going to have a political life and see if I couldn't climb the greasy pole. I knew that I was no longer afraid to challenge anyone with whom I disagreed on any issue.

The realisation had come to me that three years at the mine had significantly influenced my character and developed my confidence. After all, I had faced the dangers of earthquake and flood, snakes and wild animals, and had camped out in the African bush. I could drive a heavy vehicle over rough ground and handle a gun. As a woman in a totally male environment, I had made friends with the toughest of them without compromising my own beliefs.

As the '60s began, I was promoted to the broadcasting department at Transport House. For the first time since my days on the Odeon and Gaumont magazine I was able to offer suggestions, do some editing and take minor decisions on occasion. We had a good, well-equipped studio, with film-editing machines and closed-circuit television. Here, we recorded interviews with front-bench speakers and filmed sections to add to party political broadcasts. We also trained new candidates in the art of broadcasting.

I spent much of my free time in political activities, either at meetings of my trades union or with my local party, but I also pursued my writing and produced freelance articles for anyone who would take them. The BBC accepted two fifteen-minute pieces on life in Africa, and, for the first time since I was sixteen, I saw the inside of a radio studio. Apart from that, my publishing record seemed to be that I had written for everything – once.

The truly life-changing event for me as the new decade began was in my private life. The party had appointed a new librarian, a young graduate named Daphne Reynolds. She was a loyal and keen member of the party, and an enthusiastic supporter of the arts. We became friends and it was not long before I realised that she was gay. She even went to clubs occasionally, though she was as determined as I was to keep her private life private. When Daphne was sure she could trust me, she introduced me to some of her friends, including a former lover from her university days named Robin Morton Smith. It was love at first sight and Robin was the woman with whom I would live for six unexpected and unbelievably rich years.

Robin was head of personnel at John Lewis in Oxford Street. I had thought of John Lewis as just a useful, friendly department store, but now I began to learn how different it was when Robin told me that the staff were all partners in ownership of the store, and about the elections to the committee that she had to organise. Like any other electorate in a democracy, many of the voters were just not interested and she spent much time in encouraging them to vote for representatives to their board. The company also supported the arts – theatre, music and opera – and the staff balloted for tickets. Most of them were not interested in opera, so Robin had two tickets to Glyndebourne every year, which was a splendid perk for us.

After six months of our spending increasing amounts of time together, I suggested to Robin that we live together. To my great delight, she agreed, and we found a large top-floor flat in a big house in Islington, with a railway line at the bottom of an unloved garden.

I applied to transfer to the Islington South Labour Party and one Sunday morning there was a ring at the front door. I went down and opened it to a woman from the Labour Party, whose name I no longer remember, but our encounter remains fresh in my memory. She was the mayor, short, plump and formidable. 'Is that your car outside? The one with the CND sticker?' I said it was.

'We don't have to have you, you know.'

'Well, lots of party members are CND,' I protested, as yet unaware that the party's Islington branch was very right-wing.

'Not many I know. Do you know much about the party?'

'I should,' I replied. 'I work at Transport House.' She practically hugged me. 'Well, why didn't you say so? Are you going to make me a cup of tea?'

I was forgiven for my dangerous views; they couldn't be that dangerous if I worked at Transport House. The mayor told me about the various local party leaders, and that the council was always solid Labour. I made a note of the regular monthly meetings and she left, highly pleased with her new member.

In the following six years, life moved from one happy occasion to the next. My working life was full of positive encounters. Tony Benn kept a professional eye on our broadcasts and I learnt how to edit sound tape. I became involved in office politics and was elected to the staff committee. On evenings when I was free from local politics, Robin and I went to the theatre, or to see a film, a concert or an opera. Sadler's Wells Theatre was a favourite destination, with new operas practically on our doorstep. We learnt to love Janáček when Charles Mackerras introduced his works to London. We listened to talks beforehand and went to see works such as Janáček's *From the House of the Dead*, which are not often performed. We hated it when success moved the English National Opera from Sadler's Wells to the Coliseum, and it was a few years before we learnt to love its new home. When we weren't relishing the cultural riches on offer, we entertained our friends – and in a manner I had not done before. Robin was a fine and clever cook, and our guests dined on scallops and complicated potato dishes. Not expensive, but always delicious.

One particular day with Robin stands out in my memory. We had tickets for Glyndebourne to see Strauss's glorious *Der Rosenkavalier*. We drove there in my new Mini through the sunshine. *Punch* magazine had accepted a story of mine. I loved and was loved. I was totally happy.

In spite of the political crises which disturbed the surface of office life at Transport House, there was a fairly steady rhythm about our work, culminating each month in a meeting of the National Executive Committee. Here, all the various strands of the party met, and in the '60s the strands were even physically distinguishable: trades unionists with scarred faces and stiff hands; Oxbridge dons who spoke in educated accents with a hesitant academic manner; teachers, housewives and journalists from many different backgrounds. Whenever I had to go into the boardroom, I was always moved to see this physical manifestation of socialism, though I don't think anyone else particularly noticed it.

My ambition to enter Parliament was becoming more

credible now that my local party had asked me if I would stand for the council. This was my first venture into public politics and I wooed my electorate with passion. I already knew the nearby council estates because on one Sunday a month I collected sixpence from each of the Labour Party members who lived there. Sometimes a child would shout, 'Mum, it's the Labour,' and sometimes a mother would whisper, 'Don't tell me old man,' as I made my way along those crowded corridors, not missing a note of *Family Favourites*.

Now I knocked on every single door. I asked what I could do to improve things if I were elected. I listened and made notes. When the election came, I had the highest vote ever recorded for an Islington Council candidate, much higher even than that of the leader of the council. This, it turned out, was not a good career move. Not much canvassing was done in Islington in those days. Almost everyone voted Labour and there were more important ways of using political time, but I didn't know that. When we assembled in the ornate town hall in Upper Street, the leader said to me, 'I suppose you want to be on Housing.' I hadn't even thought about the various council committees, though I realised that housing was the most important. 'Well, we're putting you on baths and wash houses.' Know Thy Place, I thought.

Not long after this, the dear friend from the mine with

An early passport picture of Barbara – not a care in the world!

Barbara's father, William, her brother, Geoffrey, his bride, June, and June's parents

Barbara on the veranda at her house on the mine

Barbara proudly shows off her Hudson Terraplane

The famous Guy Fawkes, his eyes halves of a ping-pong ball with lights fixed behind them

Barbara in the bush near Lake Tanganyika with her .22 rifle

Barbara's gun licence

A tired and dirty Barbara after a day of chasing game

Mary, the mine nurse, and Barbara in the bush

The spitting cobra, *nyoka mkubwa*

Barbara looking across the man-made lake at the mine

La belle dame sans merci: 2001

Barbara Hoskins

SECURITY was total
Before I fell from grace
Pulled out of my orbit
By the beauty of your face.

I crossed an unmarked frontier
To a cryogenic zone
Ignoring warning systems
Propelled by love alone.

The first alert was coldness
And a greying loss of light
Communication distanced
Eternal solar night.

Command has severed contact
And cannot break my fall.
An alien cosmic body
Holds me in thrall.

Barbara Hoskins is head of information at the
Independent Broadcasting Authority, London, and
a regular broadcaster.

ABOVE LEFT Barbara, the new girl at the IBA,
at her desk

ABOVE RIGHT Barbara's poem in the *New
Scientist* (surname misspelled)

RIGHT Barbara with John Whitney and Lord
Thomson at her IBA leaving party

Harry Theobalds, head of advertising at the IBA, with Barbara at her leaving party

Rabbi Baroness Neuberger, Chancellor of Ulster University, giving Barbara her honorary doctorate

Barbara's seventy-fifth birthday party with Edward Heath

Barbara speaking at her
seventy-fifth birthday

The gang of four:
Katharine Whitehorn,
Heather Brigstocke,
Barbara and Mary Baker

With members of
Women in Advertising
and Communications,
London (WACL),
guests of Prime
Minister Thatcher

Barbara with some of the delegates at the Irish peace conference

Barbara, Stella Rimington and Professor Parveen Kumar at a Links
weekend in Venice

Barbara, a Cornish bard,
in procession at a Gorsedh

Barbara with her family

whom I'd had an affair in Africa turned up in London and took me out to lunch. I had missed him very much, and always remembered him bronzed and fit in shirt and shorts. Waiting for me at the steps of Transport House, however, was a gentleman in bowler hat and pinstripe suit, carrying a large bunch of roses. He had a taxi waiting. I took the flowers up to one of the washbasins in the ladies' lavatories and hurried back to remove him from the suspicious eyes of my colleagues. 'City uniform,' he explained. 'I have a meeting this afternoon about the mine. Hope I didn't alarm the peasants.'

As we drove to Prunier's in St James's Street, I wondered, not for the first time, whether I could perhaps have managed married life successfully after all. Once again, however, I decided that it would not have been fair. We had champagne before lunch, shared a bottle of wine and had brandy with the coffee. It was the best meal I had had since leaving Mpanda, but I had forgotten that there was a council meeting that evening. I went home by cab and had a short sleep before going to the town hall. I was told later that my intervention in the housing debate was 'er – impressive'. Perhaps it was just as well that I couldn't remember a word I'd said...

The council meetings were short, highly organised events. We had an opposition of only one, and standing orders ensured that they could only ask one question per subject, to save time. The really important meeting was the party meeting the night before. Here, policy was thrashed out and factions exposed, and it was here that I learnt an important lesson about the methods used by the hard left when fighting to impose extreme views: leave your most contentious policy until the end of the meeting when members want to go home. Raise it under 'any other business' and get your vote through when the less committed have left. It is amazing how often this works, even today.

Not long after this I faced another election. It was small, but very important. I stood for the chairmanship of the council for all Labour Party staff at Transport House, and I won. My political credentials were improving, and this, I realised, was noticed, when the new general secretary at Transport House asked me if I would like to work in his office.

He was Len Williams, a Yorkshireman who called a spade a spade. The general election was approaching and his workload had hugely increased. Would I like to be his administrative assistant? Another promotion! There was no job description; I was simply there to help Len. I was given a bewildering list of things to do, usually at a moment's notice, sometimes dealing with inconvenient party members who called without an appointment. If they were sufficiently distinguished, I would take them to be listened to by one of our growing number of keen young graduates in the policy departments. These departments were now headed by weighty men: Peter Shore, David Ennals, Tony Crosland and George Cunningham, who were respected at home and abroad.

While I was busy building up a credible political reputation, major political battles were raging between the right and the left of the party. The main dispute was about disarmament. The Campaign for Nuclear Disarmament (CND) had achieved huge support throughout the country. In 1962, Hugh Gaitskell defeated a CND vote at the party conference, no doubt remembering Nye Bevan's great phrase about not wishing to 'go naked into the council chambers of Europe'. Gaitskell then won a leadership challenge from Harold Wilson who, improbably, argued that there was room for agreement between the two sides in the argument. At that time I was an ardent supporter of CND and with, it seemed, most of the country, marched against sin. I now feel that it is a totally irrational position – unless one is a pacifist.

At the beginning of 1963, there was a crisis when, quite suddenly, Hugh Gaitskell died. He had been a passionate moderate. He deeply believed in the ideals of socialism and spoke with obvious sincerity, but he also believed in consensus wherever possible. After his death, there was a bitter battle for the leadership from which Harold Wilson emerged as the compromise leader. A similar situation

later arose in 1994, when John Smith also died quite unexpectedly and Tony Blair emerged as the new leader. As
Macmillan once replied to a journalist, 'Events, dear boy.'

I had met Wilson once or twice in Len Williams's office
and the more I saw of him, the more I liked him. He remembered everyone and called them by their name, even
me. When I learnt that he had a house in the Isles of Scilly
I decided that he must have really good taste. There was a
new energy at headquarters and we looked forward to the
coming election with new confidence. I was responsible for
our bookshop and was also given a key to the strongroom
where the party's most precious archives were stored.

The strongroom was a very special place: still, silent,
dust-free and full of a most powerful atmosphere. Old,
dark paintings were stacked there, waiting to be sent to
some distant Labour hall. Handbills called for the resigna-
tion of Asquith, or the introduction of an old-age pension.
Handwritten minutes, some signed by Ramsay MacDon-
ald, recorded far-reaching decisions from those early years
in power. I also read correspondence between the party, the
Quakers and Germany, making arrangements to receive
Jewish refugees from the Nazis. It was not true, as one
hears nowadays, that this country welcomed Jewish refugees with open arms. The Labour Party did so because they
were part of the Socialist International, and the Quakers
because they were Quakers, but few others helped. The

strongroom was a place I loved to visit whenever I had some free time. It was the beating heart of true Labour.

It was about this time I heard that my father was very ill. Before I could organise time off to visit him, he died. I went to his funeral and tried awkwardly to console his landlady-cum-partner. Looking back, I was uncomfortably aware that I was being unfair to her, especially as she gave me my mother's jewels when I was leaving. She was a good woman and I was sorry that I had not behaved more warmly towards her, but her Paris trip with Daddy had been just too much for me at the time. I thought of how much my mother would have loved to visit Paris.

Thinking about my father then brought back a special memory of a surprising evening we had enjoyed together in 1949, when the great American bass, Paul Robeson, who had been ostracised in America for his espousal of communism, was in England. My father phoned me out of the blue to say he was coming to London and had two tickets to hear Robeson sing at the Harringay Arena. Would I come with him? I certainly would, but I was astounded because Daddy was not usually keen on concerts; and, as a far-right Tory and a racist, he certainly wasn't keen on black Americans or communists. We met at Islington Underground station, Daddy in a dark suit and wearing his regimental tie. Although he was not a tall man, he had an air of authority that had never left him.

We had aisle seats at the concert, and Paul Robeson strode right past us through the auditorium to the platform. He looked wonderful, a big, tall and handsome man, with the charisma of a true star. The entire audience was enraptured, especially when he sang his most famous song, 'Ol' Man River', to end the evening. He changed the words from '…I get weary and sick of trying, I'm tired of livin' and scared of dying' to '…but I'll keep fighting until I'm dying'.

Daddy turned to me, his face suffused with pleasure and admiration, Robeson's extreme-left politics and black skin forgotten. 'That, Bobbie,' he said, 'is a true man.' And that was all that mattered.

* * *

On one or two rare occasions, when major disagreements were expected, I was asked to help take the minutes at a meeting of the National Executive. I watched in awe as powerful trades unionists made powerful arguments, and equally powerful women like Bessie Braddock (described by Shirley Williams as an earth mother), argued back. There was one occasion when Barbara Castle, who was always beautifully turned out, had clearly not had time to complete her toilette. She produced emery boards, scissors and a nail file, and performed a full manicure while listening to the discussion. The men looked disgusted, but busy Labour women had little time to make themselves presentable, and the Tory press were always delighted to use an unflattering photograph.

By 1964 it was becoming clear that a general election could not be far away. Our new leader, Harold Wilson, was often seen in the building. He had not been everyone's choice, as, when Hugh Gaitskell died so unexpectedly, many thought that the party would move left. Harold Wilson was the compromise. I very much admired our political leaders as they strived in each party for consensus among their warring groups.

As the political temperature rose, so did political differences at Transport House. The left/right divisions within the party were reflected within our staff. I worshipped all the stars. There was Bessie Braddock, a serious politician who could turn a crowded Albert Hall from breathless silence to a standing ovation. Sadly, the press never took her seriously. Barbara Castle was another politician with a fine mind and a sharp tongue. This was the last period of time of real, stirring oratory from politicians making wonderful speeches to huge crowds; the last time before television changed politics.

I was also more involved in the social life at work. One or two of the men asked me for a date but I managed to skirt round that. No one, of course, knew that I was gay. I flirted with the best of them, but there was always some sadness inside me because I felt I was a hypocrite. Our Christmas party was a great event. Most of the National Executive members attended, and before the dancing we held a cabaret. One year we performed *The Shooting of Dan McGrew* with colossal sound effects from the broadcasting section. I sang a duet with Gwyneth Dunwoody. We did so well that we were asked to repeat the evening at the Fabian Society's Christmas party.

The brightest people at Transport House generally wanted, and expected, to become MPs, although it was not always prudent to say so. For example, when George Cunningham was interviewed by members of the National Executive after he applied for the position of Commonwealth Secretary, he was regarded with suspicion (the party was often suspicious) for wanting to give up a well-paid position in the Foreign Office. Why would he want to come here for less money? he was asked. So that he could eventually go into the House, he replied. Wrong answer. He should have said 'to serve the party'. Although he was absolutely the right person – after all, he was in the Commonwealth Department of the Foreign Office – he almost didn't get the job because of his somewhat tactless honesty.

Up and down the country, constituencies were choosing their candidates for the 1964 general election. I realised that I now had a credible political CV to offer and I decided to apply. I couldn't expect to be of interest to a really safe seat. I would have to cut my teeth on a hopeless one first, and probably second and third, but if I did well I might achieve a marginal seat later on. I had good experience of public speaking as an Islington councillor, and my years at party headquarters had given me confident knowledge of our policies. When Stroud Constituency Labour Party invited me for a preliminary interview, I was ready.

I drove to Gloucestershire full of excitement. I like interviews, and I mentally rehearsed replies to every tricky question I could think of. And I knew that my West Country accent would help. There were eight of us, and we waited in a typically gloomy old room until we were called. We talked to each other in an embarrassed way, and I learnt that most of them had already been interviewed by several CLPs. I confessed that this was my first time, whereupon they commiserated with me, which I thought was rather unnecessary!

The interview was more a general 'get to know you' than a probing of my position on contentious issues. They were kind and friendly, especially the chairman, a middle-aged woman with an academic way of speaking. They were the sort of people I could happily work with. A week later I had a letter inviting me back for the final interview. There would be a shortlist of three and the interview would be rather longer than the first one. Again I drove west, knowing that this evening might change my life.

It was a really tough interview, especially on the question

of CND. I began confidently with the moral case against nuclear weapons, but began to stutter and stumble when asked several sharp questions about arms policies, defence, NATO and the morality of sheltering behind the Americans. They played devil's advocate well, and I am not a pacifist. I was asked how I would vote if a Labour government entered into a war with which I did not agree. Would I be loyal to my government? I made a sort of statement of conscience. I could not always guarantee to support the government whatever the subject, but I hoped the need to vote against would not arise very often. I was also asked about my personal political beliefs, and as I answered I felt myself straying further and further away from the Labour Party. To end the interview, the chairman told me that in the last few years Conservative Stroud had become increasingly marginal and they had some hopes of winning for Labour.

The journey back to London later that day was very different from the drive down. Going over their questions and my answers again and again, one certainty emerged: I was not really suited to party politics. To be a successful MP, one must loyally support party policies. Any good democrat knows that this means compromise. I now was aware for the first time in my life that I thoroughly disliked political compromise. I also saw that my Cornish liberalism was stronger than I had realised. I was not the loyal Labour woman I thought I was.

It was a bitter time. I had thought that a political career would be a natural development for me. I had spent years supporting left-wing parties, first Liberal then Labour. I could make a good speech and move an audience. I believed with all my heart in reform and change, and that I could play some small part in it. Now I realised that an MP's life was not for me. I wrote to the kindly CLP chairman in Stroud withdrawing my name and apologising for wasting their time. I still have her letter saying that I had been chosen. They particularly liked my honesty. Would I please reconsider? Sadly, I knew that whatever career I finally settled for, it would not be as a Member of Parliament, let alone a government minister.

The following week I talked over my disillusionment with George Cunningham. I felt a total failure. I had wasted years of my life pursuing a fantasy. His response was robust. 'Of course you haven't wasted these years. You've learnt a great deal about politics. Go into the civil service, you were made for it! Your experience will be invaluable and you'll go through their ranks like a hot knife through butter.' His Scottish voice strengthened the resonance of his encouragement.

I stayed on to work through the election, and to watch proudly as Harold Wilson arrived in Downing Street on 16 October 1964 to claim his new address and his place in history. It was clear that even with a majority of only four,

our new Prime Minister was going to be a moderniser; and so it proved. The country welcomed his new approach and rewarded him two years later with a majority of ninety-eight. His legacy became one that any Prime Minister would have been proud of: among many achievements, founding of the Open University, the end of capital punishment, the decriminalising of homosexuality AND he kept us out of the Vietnam War while still retaining friendly relations with America. Of course there were the failures too, but...

Yet I met right-wing people at parties – intelligent, informed people with a visceral loathing, even hatred on occasion, of Harold. I couldn't begin to understand their blind, unreasoning passion about a clever politician who was clearly doing good things. Later, I encountered exactly the same response to Margaret Thatcher from left-wing friends. I still do not understand their extreme emotions.

Gwyneth Dunwoody and Shirley Williams were both triumphant, and Robin gave a celebratory Sunday lunch for Chris, Meryl and Daphne, the party's librarian who had introduced us. After they left, I told Robin that I had decided to leave Transport House. She was not very encouraging. She knew that I had been depressed by the interviews in Stroud, but argued that, after all, they had offered me the chance to be a candidate – I really knew about politics and I had proved that I could win votes. To chair all the staff of a major political party shows that you've got what it takes to succeed in politics, she argued. I explained that the real problem was that I was no longer sure of my political allegiance, and I didn't believe that I could be a loyal party member. I felt as if I were just acting a part. She advised me not to be hasty, and said she would support whatever decision I made.

Transport House had become a strangely changed head-quarters now that the action had moved away. Journalists no longer crowded our steps. All interest had moved to No. 10 and Whitehall. There was no need for early morning starts and late finishes. Lunchtimes became longer and there was more leisure time for music, films and theatre. It was about this time that Robin told me she thought my nickname was a bit old-fashioned for the person I now was. It was prob-ably fine to be Bobbie when you were young, but 'you have a beautiful name and I think you should use it'. Not all my friends were happy about this – some thought it snobbish, others thought that Robin was trying to change me. If she were, it could only be an improvement, was my opinion. My family never accepted the change and my sister Sheila and many of my nieces and nephews still call me Bobbie.

Be all that as it may, I decided to become Barbara, and then I took George Cunningham's advice and applied for a job in the civil service.

CHAPTER THIRTEEN

Like most people, I was ignorant about the civil service and prejudiced against it. Unimaginative and boring, I thought. Nine-to-fivers. Careful, conventional and Conservative! Nonetheless, I applied for every press officer's job that came up and eventually secured a post as assistant press officer (science) at the Department of Education and Science. I was thirty-nine, and my knowledge of science stopped at School Certificate biology, but I soon discovered that I would be doing well if I took telephone messages accurately. Once again, at nearly forty, I was starting a new career – at the bottom. It was not exactly back to the typing pool, but not very much better.

The department was an unhappy union of the immensely grand and ancient Department of Education and the Science Research Council. On my first day I arrived in

Curzon Street well before nine. I went to the public enquiry office because I had been given no instructions other than to ask for Dr Jacobson, the chief information officer (Science).

'What office did you say?'

'The science press office.'

'Can't say I've heard of that one … have we got a science office here?' the smart young woman on the desk asked her colleague.

'That'll be those people on the first floor now. Ask the switchboard.'

A few minutes later, 'Are you the science press office…? Well, there's a young lady here for a job with you … Oh, all right … He says you're to wait here.'

So I lit a cigarette (those were the days), and waited in the busy enquiry office while the public came in and out to ask about schools, teacher training, university courses and overseas opportunities, and the staff gave out information and leaflets with great efficiency.

When ten o'clock had been and gone, I asked if the very civil servant would ring Dr Jacobson again.

'He says he's coming, dear.'

Half an hour later, a tall, plump, dark-haired man, wearing big spectacles, a navy suit and a worried smile, hurried in. 'You must be Barbara, I'm Geoffrey Jacobson. How do you do?' he said, as we shook hands. He was softly spoken.

'We're in a bit of a muddle, I'm afraid,' he went on, and handed me a couple of pound notes. 'We're having a leaving party for your predecessor at twelve. Would you buy some flowers for me to give her? My office is on the first floor; follow the signs to office number 104. Oh, and you'll be in 109.'

As I walked along Curzon Street, looking for a flower shop, I felt like running away. It was many years since I had been treated like an office girl and I was angry and hurt. I was an ex-councillor, a possible parliamentary candidate on first-name terms with Cabinet ministers. Then I reflected that Geoffrey Jacobson didn't know that. I had been recruited as an assistant press officer, and that was that; and, after jumping over all those civil service hurdles to get in, I was not going to get out – yet.

The flowers bought, I had a cup of coffee and wandered back through the immense entrance to my new life, past walls strong and thick enough to repulse a tank. Later I learnt that our building used to house MI5 – or was it MI6? Something pretty secret anyway.

I waved to the enquiry staff in the foyer and began the search for room 104 with my armful of flowers. On the way I passed room 109. The door was open; there was laughter and the clink of wine glasses.

At 104 I knocked, waited, knocked again and walked in. Dr Jacobson looked up from a desk piled with books and papers. 'It's a bit chaotic here I'm afraid, there's a report I have to finish … Oh, the flowers, thank you. Come with me, I'll introduce you. We'll have a proper talk later.'

We returned to 109 – 'my' office – which I learnt was the general office where two typists and the assistant press officer – now me – lived, and where journalists waited for their appointments. There were three desks. Mine was in the middle, opposite the door. I met my predecessor, a pretty young woman who was getting married, and I was introduced to Charles, the principal information officer, Alan, the senior information officer, and the typists. Speeches were made, of both farewell and welcome. My flowers were presented. By two o'clock I was alone with the typists, and that was when my briefing began.

The typists soon became friends. One was a middle-aged widow named Maria. She explained that she had taken the job to be near Harrods because her 'real' work was cooking for rich families. After telephoning her client to discuss the menu, she spent her long lunchtimes shopping in Harrods's magnificent food hall. When she staggered back, she delighted in showing me what she'd bought, and discussing cooking methods and the tastes of her clients. She had three regulars for whom she cooked dinner parties and sometimes lunch.

'But what if they clash?' I asked. 'I can usually work something out. They all live fairly near each other in St

John's Wood, and I have a flat in Swiss Cottage and a little car. Sometimes I prepare the main course the day before.' I loved our long conversations. I'd never seen such expensive food close up, the luxury-filled packages even leaning against my desk on occasion.

The other typist, Clare, was tall and dark with a fine, slim body and a beautiful, low voice. She had read English Literature at Durham, where she managed to achieve a 2:1, even though she spent most of her time acting. From university she had gone straight into rep theatre. Now in her forties, she explained that she had found theatrical life in the provinces just too tiring.

'All those bed-and-breakfast digs, always on the move. The West End didn't want me and, besides, I wanted a decent home and a cat, so when my mother died…'

Clare loved English literature and grammar fiercely, and was appalled by the work she received from Charles and Alan. Sometimes she read aloud from their drafts. 'Barbara,' she would say, 'Why can't science be described in decent English? Just listen to this!'

I was only too happy to listen. I also made sure that I translated the work which came my way into comprehensible and, if possible, simple English for my draft press notices. But the scientists who telephoned from their research laboratories, or sometimes even turned up in our office, complained.

'It's too broad a brush ... you must explain that there are exceptions or modifications ... what if my colleagues see this...?'

'It's pretty unlikely, unless they are journalists,' I would reply. 'This is for the general media. We're arranging a special conference for you to talk to the scientific press, plus a meeting with *Nature*.'

'Oh, all right, but there is another thing. Which paper should I buy to read about it?'

I was amazed. 'There is no guarantee that any of this will be used. If there's a big news story it might not get a line anywhere, though *The Times* or the *Telegraph* might give it a paragraph.'

'But this is a government announcement!' It was the turn of the scientists to be amazed, and some of them returned to their laboratories deeply disillusioned with the press office.

If Clare was in a good mood she would rewrite the worst transgressions, and Charles and Alan were amused and grateful. Our press releases had to be approved by Dr Jacobson, the only educated man there, according to Clare. He liked my work and soon began to trust me. He looked as if he should have been a jolly, easy-going man, but he was always in a state of extreme anxiety.

We were a small, quite vertical hierarchy. Our chief, Dr Jacobson, was a distinguished Cambridge physicist;

Charles, a Glaswegian, had a MSc in Physics, while Alan had left school at sixteen and worked on local papers in Hammersmith. I was the junior addition to this triumvirate.

Charles and Alan would wander in and out of the general office to chat to Clare, gossip and check on what I was up to. My work came via Dr Jacobson and they were curious to see how I would do. I don't think they ever really saw Maria, except to give her typing.

The first ministerial press conference after I joined the department was organised very differently from those at Transport House, where I had been used to great informality. The political journalists were often old friends of the politicians and the atmosphere was relaxed. At Curzon Street I checked the journalists in, made a note of their names and their newspapers or broadcasting companies, and handed them a press notice. Dr Jacobson and Charles escorted the minister to the platform and sat either side of him. A carafe of water and tumblers had been placed on the table earlier – by me – together with paper and pencils. The atmosphere was very formal. Charles identified the questioners by name and quietly told the minister whom to beware of.

After the minister and Dr Jacobson left, the journalists crowded to the back of the hall where Charles and Alan were opening bottles. Charles took me on one side. 'Your job, wee Barbara, is to collect every bottle when the press have gone and take them to my room. Every last bottle, mind!'

He then explained to the journalists in more detail the ministerial announcement, translating the latest scientific breakthrough into demotic English.

When the last journalist had gone, I returned to the general office, borrowed Maria's shopping bag and clinked my way to Charles's office. He and Alan were waiting. 'Put them down here … that's right … no more phone calls to us today …' As I left, I heard him lock the door! For the rest of the afternoon I took press calls. If they were too technical I asked Dr Jacobson to ring the caller back. Maria made us tea and Clare did the *Times* crossword or read one of her densely worded novels with long paragraphs. Soon after four o'clock, Maria left. I had often wondered how she fitted in her catering work with a nine-to-five job and the answer was she didn't: she worked from ten until four. There was no supervision of the science unit at all.

My greatest excitement was when I wrote the first press notice on holography. Dr Jacobson explained the principle of laser beams to me. He was a great teacher, patient and clear. He illustrated on graph paper what he meant by a coherent light source and I wrote about it with patriotic pride. The somewhat lackadaisical attitude around the department worked to my advantage. Charles and Alan seemed deeply unengaged with work. They were amused at my interest and encouraged me to draft press notices.

Dr Jacobson was never too busy to explain our work to

me. I started reading the *New Scientist* which, he told me, most scientists read because it was written in layman's language and they didn't understand work outside their own disciplines. Years later, I wrote a regular column on science broadcasting in the *New Scientist*, and even had a poem published in it once – the only time they had published a poem. I like to think Dr Jacobson would have approved.

One or two of the journalists we dealt with were science graduates and Charles went for long lunches with them. Alan lunched with journalists from the *Mirror* and the *News of the World*, and I doubt they discussed much science. They would return from their respective outings, happily mellow, and tell us about the restaurants they had visited. Maria was always interested but they really wanted to talk to Clare, who kept her distance as much as possible. They tried in vain to impress her. Charles invited her out to lunch, but he knew nothing of the arts, she told me, and so she turned him down.

As I grew more accustomed to the science office, I became aware that there were senior beings above us: not only the minister himself, but the permanent secretary, who had a knighthood and who sometimes lunched with Dr Jacobson. Late one afternoon when the others had gone, the phone rang.

'This is Sir Richard. Can you come to my office?'

He gave me directions, and for the first time I took the lift which, until then, had been for Education staff only.

'Come in. How do you do?' We shook hands and I sat opposite him across an imposing desk. 'What is your name? Ah, yes, you're from Transport House. It must seem rather different here, I expect ... Do you like it?'

I told him I liked it very much and had had no idea of the tremendous work of British science, especially in the field of lasers. Sir Richard smiled, and held up a piece of paper which I recognised immediately – a piece on British scientific achievements that I had been drafting for Dr Jacobson. 'Did you draft this?' he asked. I nodded. 'Ah ... it's not bad, but you really must mention Dragon. It can't be complete without that. Why did you leave it out?'

'Well, I felt I couldn't put everything in,' was my off-the-cuff reply. I could hardly say I'd never heard of Dragon.

'What did you say your name was?' Sir Richard asked, with a piercing look. 'Thank you. We will meet again.'

I went back to my office and wondered how to find out about Dragon. There were a few dog-eared reference books from which I chose *Whitaker*'s as a start ... Sadly, neither the reference books nor my colleagues appeared to have heard of Dragon, and I never did find out.

Gradually, my press notices became more professional: broad-brush in the first paragraph with more detail in the subsequent text. Sometimes I was allowed to write eye-catching headlines, something that reminded me of my cinema publicity days and that I particularly enjoyed

– for example, 'How're They Going to Keep Them Down on the Farm?' announced a scheme to encourage agricultural workers to attend a scientific festival in Paris.

My favourite memory of my early days in the civil service is of the first time I was given responsibility for taking science correspondents to Scotland. By then I was on first-name terms with most of them, and there were two whom I particularly liked, Colin Riach at the BBC, and Angela Croome with the *Daily Telegraph* and the *New Scientist*. They were both extremely good at their work and asked some very difficult questions. At least I now knew whom to put them in touch with, and they were patient with me as I learnt my way around the great world of British science.

I had been greatly looking forward to flying to Edinburgh with my group, staying at a smart hotel in Princes Street and accompanying them to Scottish science laboratories. All went well until we arrived at the hotel. 'Where is the bar?' asked the *Times* journalist. The bewhiskered receptionist looked amazed. 'There is no bar here, sir. This is a temperance hotel.' The journalists roared with laughter. 'That was a wonderful joke, Barbara. Now where IS our hotel?'

I was appalled and mortified. I had never heard of a temperance hotel. I had certainly never met one in Cornwall, and I didn't know what to do. It was too late to find another hotel for eight people that night.

Colin comforted me. 'Don't look so upset Barbara, the doorman is most obliging. He is used to this problem and he's already quietly making arrangements in our rooms. See him separately about the bill – and for God's sake do it quietly.' The situation was thus saved, and the story of Barbara's temperance hotel preceded me back to Curzon Street, where it did me no harm at all.

The work of the Science department, an arm of the Department of Education, occasionally overlapped with the newly created MinTech, the Ministry of Technology, where Barbara Castle was the minister, and which had its own information officers. Dr Jacobson told me there was to be a joint press conference, 'And it has to be held here, not at Millbank.' He seemed quite excited about it.

We worked most happily together on the preparations. Much time was spent on the composition of the top table: two ministers, two senior information officers, who else …? ('Perhaps not you, Charles.') On the day all went smoothly. There were enough copies of the press handouts, the microphones worked, the ministers and the press were pleased, and I met my opposite number from MinTech. There was one mildly awkward moment for me when Barbara Castle said, 'Hello Barbara, what are you doing here?' and wished me good luck, which raised a few eyebrows.

The chief information officer at MinTech was Harold Winterbourne, a relaxed character with a ready smile and a kindly manner. He was coming up for retirement and had seen it all before.

'How do you like it here?' he asked me. 'Rather different from your last job, I imagine?'

'Not so very different, same cast list of ministers at the moment. Very different ways of working though.'

'I'm sure.' He looked around him with an expression of disapproval. 'This isn't the real civil service, you know; don't be deceived by first impressions. It's nice to meet you, Barbara. I hear good things about you.' My surprise showed and Mr Winterbourne smiled. 'From the press.' I hadn't realised until then that the same group of journalists also covered MinTech.

Not long after that joint press conference, I had a phone call from Harold Winterbourne. 'There is a vacancy in my office for an assistant press officer. You could apply for a sideways move if you'd like to, and you'll be promoted within four months.'

I thought about it. I really liked Dr Jacobson and I was learning a great deal about science, but I couldn't help him with his management problems. Charles and Alan were wholly disaffected and there was a sad feeling around the office.

Where was the personnel office? I asked Clare. 'You mean Estabs. We hardly ever speak to them. They are, of course, Education.'

I spoke to Dr Jacobson. 'Typical Harold, he's poaching! Can't blame him. I can't get you promotion here, though you deserve it.' His voice sounded hopeless. 'I'll miss you, but of course you must go.'

Flowers were produced at my farewell party – I don't know who bought them this time. Charles and Alan made for the bottles. I promised to keep in touch with Maria and Clare, but I didn't. And on to my next chapter I went.

CHAPTER FOURTEEN

It was exhilarating to move from a red-brick fortress in Curzon Street to post-war Millbank Tower. I was taken up to the eighth floor and shown into an open-plan office where five men sat at large desks. I, too, was given a large desk and comfortable chair, but no telephone. A slip-up somewhere, I was told. 'You'll have one tomorrow … can't have a press officer without a phone.' I had a wonderful view over the Thames to the west.

My welcome was unenthusiastic. It was the first time there had been a woman in the press office, and they told me later they were worried that they would have to mind their speech and behaviour. I also learnt that not everyone approved of the civil service's equal pay policy. I saw with satisfaction that my male colleagues were all about my age, and later learnt that three were family men with young children, one was married with no children and one was divorced and single.

One winter's day when we were preparing to leave, there was a superb sunset over the river. 'Oh, look at that sunset,' I exclaimed. 'Come over here, it really is stunning.' Grudgingly, one came, and gradually the others joined us to admire a beautiful ending to the day. Thus, slowly, they became friendly although they still behaved in a very macho way when they were all together.

The work of the Ministry of Technology was divided up between us. One had Concorde, another had satellites and so forth. I was given to the hovercraft project. The senior information officer and the principal gave me background reading and arranged for my first visit to the research station near Cowes on the Isle of Wight. I was also told the story of how the project had begun with a radio engineer, boat builder and inventor named Christopher Cockerell.

Cockerell wanted to create enough energy to lift objects off the ground, and had been experimenting with a weight-bearing cushion of air for fifteen years. He had then applied for a grant to continue his experiments and the civil servant who was responsible for approving this grant invited him in to give a demonstration. They met in a small committee room and sat on a table while a green Lyons coffee tin glided over the carpet under their feet. At that stage it was not at all clear how this power pack could be applied commercially, but the civil servant, smitten as everyone was by the idea of this weird invention, allocated sufficient money for Christopher Cockerell to continue with its development. By the time I arrived at MinTech, a hovercraft was bounding above the waves near the Isle of Wight.

Once more I was enjoying being a tiny part of British scientific life. I accompanied the press to the National Physical Laboratory at Teddington, where many of our great achievements have begun. I saw the wind tunnels where the stability of the New York World Trade Center was tested. It was strong enough to survive a hurricane but not, alas, the 9/11 terrorist attack that would befall it in 2001. It was here that the bouncing bombs were tested and I couldn't resist telling the staff showing me around that Wing Commander Guy Gibson, who led the Dambusters, was educated in the kindergarten at my school in Penzance: the only girls' school to boast a holder of the Victoria Cross!

I also enjoyed the continuity of working with the science press, particularly Colin Riach, the BBC science correspondent who had come to the rescue at the temperance hotel in Edinburgh, and Angela Croome of the *Daily Telegraph*, who wrote about science in such elegant English. Angela remained a close friend until her death, and I wrote the obituary for her newspaper.

One of our press officers, Frank Osborne, who worked on air shows, spent long lunch hours drinking in the pub in Smith Square, which I knew well from Transport House days. One afternoon our principal came in asking for him. 'He's gone up to see Mr Williams. On the eighteenth floor I think,' I said. 'Well, tell him I want to see him when he gets back.'

My colleagues were surprised and pleased that I had protected Frank. 'Is there a Mr Williams?' they asked. 'There is always a Mr Williams,' I answered.

When Frank came back he was grateful and also surprised, and from then on I was fully accepted as one of the team.

Not long afterwards, as Mr Winterbourne had predicted, a note came round announcing a vacancy for an information officer. I applied, was interviewed by a board of three, and won my first promotion. I bought chocolate cakes for the press office, and that evening Robin took me out to celebrate at Mon Plaisir in Seven Dials, our favourite French restaurant. It is still there, as lovely and as French as ever.

As hovercraft trials continued, it was decided to take the science press out to sea so that they could watch her being put through her paces. We went to Southampton where a large boat was waiting to take us into the Solent. A cloud of spray announced the hovercraft's approach and I wished I had told the press to wear mackintoshes. Angela with her naval background was well equipped to watch from the rail. Some of the others retreated below to the bar where they read the information I had written. The coverage next day, with some dashing pictures, was good and Mr Winterbourne was pleased. I settled in happily at MinTech, hardly aware that Barbara Castle had been succeeded by Tony Benn. My status was very far below theirs!

In time I visited most of the government research stations. I watched fires being ignited and extinguished, and I saw thousands of flies in a bottle – they smelt dreadful. I watched communications with satellites, and research on rubber tank tracks. I especially enjoyed a by-product of this work, some unusual rubber balls, arranged in boxes of two, in which they looked identical. Drop them, and one would fall like lead and remain where it was; the other would bounce up and down like mad from floor to ceiling. I believe the scientists never found a use for them.

The hovercraft project prospered and British Rail, which already operated ship ferries, became interested in the possibility of a cross-channel service. There were trials on the Thames, and the public welcomed this novel form of transport. Other uses for the hover principle were investigated: perhaps hospital patients with burns could float on a jet of air ... perhaps the terrific noise in mills could be reduced by floating the bobbins on air. Everyone seemed to be excited by the possibilities. The media were full of stories.

The opening of the cross-channel service was celebrated royally. The Duke of Edinburgh had already driven a craft on trials – so fast that the bows acquired what was known as the 'Royal Dent'. Now Princess Anne joined the inaugural flight, escorted by our minister, Tony Benn, and a group of British and French dignitaries. They drank champagne behind a cloud of spray and toasted Christopher Cockerell, now Sir Christopher.

The next day, it was the turn of the media to have their trip across the Channel and celebrate at a ceremony in Calais. We set out for Southampton at nine o'clock and British Rail gave us generous hospitality on our journey. We boarded our craft and admired the smooth, fast flight over the sea. In Calais we were shown into a large hall where we saw a promising array of bottles, and tables laid for a feast. We were welcomed by the mayor, but no drinks were forthcoming. The French, it appeared, would not open the bottles until the food had arrived. The always resourceful Colin Riach quietly purloined a bottle of champagne and we disappeared under a huge linen table cloth, surfacing again when wonderful aromas told us the food had arrived.

For some years there was a regular cross-channel service, and an attempt was made to introduce a service on the Thames, but gradually it became obvious that technical difficulties seemed to make hovercraft too expensive for normal commercial work. It is a pity that the great hopes for a hovercraft future were never fully realised. It proved too unwieldy as well as too costly for major commercial success, but it still has its uses in special situations. For instance, in 1969 Sir Ranulph Fiennes reached the source of the Nile by hovercraft. Today they still fly over ice and snow in Canada and float over jungles in Indonesia, and there is a regular daily service to the Isle of Wight where it all began.

I occasionally saw Tony Benn at press conferences, where he always greeted me warmly. After all, it was only three years since we had both been working at Transport House though, of course, things were very different now. Tony was in the government, running a ministry; I was on the bottom rung of a new career ladder. I wondered sometimes where I would have been if I had stayed in politics. Robin and many friends missed my stories of the larger-than-life politicians who once came to my office, but were rather less interested in my immersion in science. There was one occasion when I was asked to accompany Tony Benn to a conference in Cardiff. We travelled by plane with his private secretary, Robin Lingard. To my surprise they began arguing about who should fly the plane. They had both been in the University Air Squadron and wanted the pilot to let them take the controls. They became really angry with each other – no 'Yes, Minister' about this private secretary! In those days there were many more cross-connections between politicians and civil servants, who often knew each other from school and university, than there seem to be today. I think it made the implementation of government policies much smoother.

When hovercraft ceased to be of such direct government interest, I was transferred to work with a touring exhibition. It was an attempt to educate small manufacturing businesses in modern methods. A huge double-decker bus had been fitted out with examples of cheaper, more efficient ways to manufacture. In the '60s there were thousands of very small factories where, for example, hours were still spent resharpening and reusing machine tool tips. My exhibition was to encourage them to throw these tips away and use new ones instead of sharpening them again. It seems extravagant but it actually saved money. Downstairs in the bus were examples of different methods of drilling and cutting metal, while upstairs was a cinema where educational films were shown to reinforce the message. I arranged opening ceremonies with the local mayor, the chairmen of local business groups and, of course, the media, as I followed the bus across the UK.

On my pay grade I stayed in boarding houses, where supper was at six-thirty sharp and there was nothing to eat if you turned up late. I met some very unrewarding travelling salesmen in these establishments, and some formidable landladies. My biggest excitement was when we went to Belfast and the bus fell into a lough. The *Belfast Telegraph* had a headline, 'Barbara Makes a Splash', and gave our message front-page treatment. The permanent legacy for me from touring with the exhibition was that I read the whole of Proust's *À La Recherche du Temps Perdu* – all twelve volumes – twice. I went to the art gallery in every town we visited and I have always been grateful to MinTech for that.

Soon after I entered my third year in the civil service, I applied for a vacancy at the Department of the Environment (DoE) for a senior information officer. I was successful, and exchanged my friends on the eighth floor with the spectacular view for three concrete slabs a stone's throw from Transport House.

DoE was the ugliest building in London. Three oblong slabs, twelve floors high, sat in a row, their windows either looking at each other or at nearby office blocks. It was a post-war failure, built on a bombsite. It was not even a convenient building: we wasted much time going up and down from office to office. And as well as being the ugliest, it was the biggest department of government, with twelve ministers under a Secretary of State, and covered housing, local government, roads, rail and aviation. It also had the biggest information department, with a director, several principals and even more senior information officers – of which I was now one – with my own office!

I hated my first assignment. One of the most important and newsworthy activities in the department was fixing the precept (allocation of money) for local government spending. This was done in conjunction with the Treasury, and laid down the amounts of money town halls could spend in the new financial year. It was immensely complicated and I never really understood it, although I had to attempt to explain details to journalists. Fortunately, my principal did most of the briefing, leaving me to just muddle through with the most hopeless journalists on minor provincial newspapers.

It was fortunate that I could hide within a group of more experienced colleagues because my personal life was becoming difficult, too. For some time I had been aware that my relationship with Robin was becoming cooler. We sometimes spent evenings with other people and I had been away a great deal with that bus. I had not realised how serious the rift had become. One evening, Robin told me she'd arranged for us to go out to the Bell at Aston Clinton for Sunday lunch with our friend Ann. I looked forward to it – excellent food and lovely countryside. We went in my car, picking up Ann on the way. She was always good company, and I loved hearing about her work as one of the top film editors in the country.

After an extravagant meal, Robin asked me to go for a walk with her while Ann ordered coffee. Then she held my hand and told me that she wanted to leave me and wanted to live with Ann, but that she didn't want to lose my friendship. She would always love me, but Ann had become overwhelmingly important to her. Her words were a deep shock. She could not have been kinder in telling me, but I had had no idea that Ann was any more than a friend and I was stunned as well as deeply wounded. My feelings for Robin were profound and tenacious. I had loved before, several times, but not on so many levels. I could not imagine a life without her. She said it would not be without her. She would be there.

We wept, blew our noses and returned to the restaurant. Ann kissed me and said how grateful she was that I had taken the news so well. Looking back now, I know I did behave well, but I could have done no other. I do not think my feelings were obsessional. They were certainly deep, and it must have been difficult sometimes for Ann when so often, to borrow the words of the old music hall song, Barbara came too.

Troubles never come singly, and I found that I was also in trouble at work. The huge DoE included the old Department of Public Buildings and Works. My chief press officer asked me if I could generate some publicity for our public buildings. They included some lovely houses, such as Audley End, and there was an annual membership card which secured admission to all of them for one pound. I thought hard. It was coming up to Christmas and this card would make a lovely and cheap Christmas present.

I rang Biddy Baxter at the BBC and asked her whether *Blue Peter* might be interested. The children who watched her programme might like to give their mummies and daddies the membership card as a Christmas present, I suggested. Biddy liked the idea, and a week later there was a five-minute piece with lovely pictures of Audley End, a large picture of the card and the address of the DoE. I was pleased with this publicity and hoped the public buildings department would be, too.

A few days later I was summoned by a furious under-secretary. 'What have you done?' he yelled. 'We are receiving thousands and thousands of letters every day for this damned membership card. I have had to move staff in from other departments to deal with the post. Work is being held up!'

I apologised and explained that I had been asked to improve the take-up of the cards. 'Yes, but not like this!' I apologised again and crept back to my office where the chief press officer was waiting. 'It's like a friend who has asked to help with the washing-up and then breaks all your dishes,' he explained. 'You have a tendency, Barbara, to exceed your brief.'

Later, I learnt that the minister responsible for public buildings had been congratulated by friends on the membership cards their children had given them and he was delighted, but by that time I had stopped worrying about the DoE. My civil service life was about to change yet again.

CHAPTER FIFTEEN

My unexpected transfer in 1970 from the DoE to No. 10 Downing Street was not through open competition. The usual system of applying for a vacancy and being interviewed in competition with others did not apply – in those days, at any rate. At No. 10 a system of who you knew operated, as it does so often elsewhere. In my case, Janet Hewlett-Davies, an excellent press officer who worked at No. 10 with the Prime Minister's press secretary, Joe Haines, introduced me to him at a party.

Joe Haines knew that I had worked at Transport House. After we had gossiped for a while about Labour people, Joe asked whether I would be interested should there be a vacancy for a senior information officer in the Prime Minister's press office. Would I?! I would have walked to work barefoot for such a job. It might not happen, Joe warned.

It would mean an extra member of staff and he might not be able to make a case for it. I was amazed. Surely if the PM wanted an extra press officer he got one, but it wasn't as simple as that. There were establishment numbers to be considered. I left Joe Haines in no doubt as to my enthusiasm and commitment, and as I left the party, Janet told me she desperately needed someone to share the load, and hoped to be working with me.

Until that conversation I had looked forward to every day at Environment. I thoroughly enjoyed my work and my colleagues, and in such a big department each day brought something new and different. Now there was the possibility of something infinitely more interesting and I was hugely excited. Days turned into weeks with no word from Joe Haines, and gradually daily problems resumed their urgency.

At last a civil service letter arrived at home asking me to attend an interview in Bloomsbury to check my suitability for No. 10. I dreaded it. Would my boisterous days of clubs and pubs in Chelsea be examined? Were my politics too left-wing? Thankfully, it soon became clear that my past late nights were not considered particularly wild. I had never even smoked marijuana. More interesting was a long discussion about CND, which expanded into talking about the nature of the Labour Party and communist influence. 'Methodism and Marxism', as Morgan Phillips memorably put it when he argued that Labour was strongly rooted in Methodism. It was an exhilarating experience.

Not long afterwards, Henry James, the chief information officer at the DoE, summoned me to his office. 'I've had a call from No. 10. For some reason they want you over there.' I said nothing. 'I don't want you to go,' he went on. 'You're doing a good job here, and I must remind you that information staff have no home department. You may not be able to come back to us later on.'

'But surely it's a great opportunity to learn?' I said.

'Well, Joe Haines is only a temporary civil servant and his ways are not ours...' He stopped there, obviously realising that I was wild with excitement. 'Well, good luck,' he said. 'You'll start very soon.'

*   *   *

It was only a few days after this that I received joining instructions to report at ten o'clock the following Monday morning.

On the day, I walked up Downing Street and coincided with a group of tourists about to photograph the front door and the solitary policeman outside guarding it. I felt embarrassed to push past them, and waited until they had moved off towards Horse Guards Parade. The policeman asked me in a friendly Scottish voice for my name and told me to knock on the august door.

I recognised the entrance hall from a previous visit when the staff of Transport House had been invited to a party to celebrate the general election, and also from television pictures of Prime Ministers shaking hands with their guests in front of a big fireplace. A uniformed member of staff said, 'I believe you are for the press office. This way.' How did he know? I followed him along a corridor and into what I recognised with relief as a press office: overflowing piles of papers on chairs and tables; Janet on the phone; Joe with his jacket off, talking to someone at the end of a long table. Janet waved, Joe smiled. 'Welcome Barbara … can't stop. George, this is Barbara.' He disappeared into a large room with windows looking on to Downing Street.

I was welcomed by George Holt, the principal information officer. He was a career civil servant nearing retirement, very formal in his speech and writing. He was not happy about the informality with which Janet and I talked to journalists. 'But we know them, George,' we'd say, when he suggested we were lowering the tone of the office. He always answered the phone with 'The Prime Minister's press office here, Mr George Holt speaking.' He was immensely hard-working and researched endless facts and dates for Joe's morning briefings, afterwards following up with more background information on questions which had arisen. Joe, the quick, tough, ex-political editor of the *Daily Mirror*, treated George with careful politeness, explaining his needs in much more detail than his shouted requests to us.

The press office in those days was a large room dominated by a beautiful old table, its deeply polished surface pitted with the weight of heavy typewriters. George sat at one end and there were piles of newspapers at the other. Janet and I sat opposite one another on either side. There were several telephones, internal and external directories and wire baskets for incoming and outgoing post. For me the beauty of our work was that, generally, it was so immediate. Every call, perhaps with a follow-up call for additional information, was a task completed. Almost all enquiries were from political journalists often requesting only a date or name, but sometimes a call could turn into a long policy briefing – particularly if the journalist was from a regional paper.

There were no facilities for lunch, and most staff brought sandwiches which they ate at their desks in winter and in the park when the weather grew warmer. George always went out; Joe would lunch in the press gallery at the House of Commons on the rare occasions when he was not the guest of a journalist or editor. When it was very busy, Doris, a permanent member of the No. 10 staff, and responsible for our clerical support, fed us unlimited tea and coffee. She was very down-to-earth. Recruited straight from secretarial school, Doris had seen many great men come and go, and enjoyed telling us stories about Churchill's deafness and the old deaf butler who looked after him at No. 10 dinners. The butler had painful feet and would cry aloud, 'Why can't they all go home?'

In between calls, we read everything we could find. George threw a fat file over to me. 'This is prepared by the Society of Genealogists,' he explained. 'They give us a family tree for all incoming Prime Ministers, and then we add to it.'

I saw what he meant. In addition to the Wilson family marriages and offspring, going back through many generations, there was a ragbag of current information – the PM's shoe size, for example. It's very detailed because you never know what might be asked for, especially by foreign journalists. They were looked after by the Foreign Office, but we also received many unusual questions from them.

Gradually I became used to going through the front door, and could confidently find my way around the main offices. I learnt that the Scottish policeman who had first welcomed me was a poet, who wrote in a much-loved Scottish dialect known as Lallans – and that the switchboard were the most dedicated group in No. 10, and gave the very best Christmas party. These ladies, who made and received calls to world leaders everywhere, were hugely intelligent and very responsible, as well as fashionably dressed and made-up despite being hidden from public view. They liked my Cornish accent, which pleased me no end. That was how communications were way back in the '70s.

One evening when things were quiet, Janet took me to see the Cabinet room and its library. There is a tradition that every Cabinet minister on retirement should give one of his books to No. 10. I looked at some of them, heavy tomes on economic or foreign policy, each signed and dated, but a few books of poetry, too, including one by Enoch Powell.

Every morning there was a meeting in Joe Haines's beautiful room with the Lobby correspondents. This was the group of political journalists who had special privileges. Everything Joe said was off the record, and this convention was usually honoured. These briefings enabled Joe to announce the PM's diary and give the background to that day's political stories. George Holt always accompanied Joe, and Janet and I took turns at sitting in.

Prime Minister's Questions were twice a week in those days, and afterwards there was a briefing in the House, in the offices reserved for political journalists. The Palace of Westminster turns into a rabbit warren if you climb the stairs away from the wide corridors and grand public rooms. In the early days I often lost my way as I puffed from floor to floor with the latest hot press release. These meetings at the House were conducted by the Lobby chairman and we were there as guests. The basis of our relationship with the press was one of absolute trust. We relied on them never to quote us and they relied on the honesty and accuracy of our information. Similarly, the whole of No. 10 worked on the basis of trust. Once inside that door, you were treated as one of the family. As press officers, Janet and I absorbed as much information as we could on every current topic. Then, during the odd lull in activity, we talked cooking and theatre, exchanged recipes and became lifelong friends.

Occasionally there was an overseas visit. Janet accompanied Harold Wilson to the Far East and came back with two orchids for me. When Mr Wilson became Prime Minister in 1964, his first visit was to Washington for talks with President Lyndon Johnson. He naturally wanted Marcia Williams, his political secretary, to accompany him. The story runs that Marcia went to see the PM's principal private secretary to discuss the visit. 'I'm not sure how we're going to include you,' she was told. Then, a few days later, 'Don't worry, I've fixed it. You can go as Mrs Wilson's maid.' I was told that the volcanic eruption which followed was the first time the private office had experienced Marcia's hurt and anger. If the story was true, I felt she had every right to be angry and insulted. She was a well-educated graduate, an acute politician to her polished fingertips and she had every right to her position as the Prime Minister's political secretary. The civil servants were arrogant. Was it because she was the first woman to hold that position? It should not be forgotten that Marcia Williams was one of those first few women who pushed open the door through which so many other women have followed.

* * *

My friends were impressed with my new position. What was it like? they wondered. Rather odd, I thought, because I had never been in a place where everything was so totally dominated by one man. Although I rarely saw Harold Wilson, I knew, as did every member of the staff, where he was and what he was doing almost all the time. The whole building reacted to him and seemed to relax only when the front door closed on his retreating back.

One Saturday afternoon when I knew the PM was at Chequers and unlikely to appear, I took Robin to look round the famous establishment. She was gratifyingly impressed when the duty policeman greeted me by name and when my knock was answered immediately. I ushered Robin inside, where she lowered her voice as if in church as she looked around the hall, but perked up when she saw the press office. 'What's that painting behind your chair?' 'That's an Elisabeth Frink.' I explained that ministers chose art works for their private offices from the government art collection, and that, at No. 10, every room, even the general press office, was hung with fine British art.

As soon as Joe felt that I could be trusted with evening duty, I was added to the rota. Janet was relieved because she and George had worked every other week; now we each worked one week in three. Being on duty meant staying at home throughout the evening and taking calls put through by the No. 10 switchboard. Usually there weren't many, other than Lobby journalists fact-checking, but sometimes foreign broadcasters rang in the middle of the night. There was one from Radio Sydney wondering why the British loved Australian comedians like Dame Edna and Basil Brush. I wasn't too keen on being woken up for that discussion. There was only one occasion when I was deliberately unhelpful. We all felt very strongly about apartheid, so I didn't welcome being woken by a call from South Africa; and when a very Afrikaner voice said, 'This is Radio Durban. You're on the air!' I replied, 'Oh, no, I'm not,' and hung up.

All through the spring of 1970, speculation about an election excited all the journalists and staff, except Doris. 'It will give you lots of free time,' she said, and I realised that, as a neutral civil servant, particularly at No. 10, I could hardly be politically active. The date of the election was announced for 18 June. I had not previously realised the solemnity and beauty of the proclamation. A copy was fixed to the gates of Horse Guards, and I marvelled at the majestic grammatical progress from 'Whereas' through to the end of a long paragraph.

Doris was right. We had weeks of nothing to do while Joe went off with the PM and all the political journalists left Westminster. It was an unreal time of long lunch hours in the park in beautiful weather, then devouring all the newspapers, radio and TV reports. We were sure that Mr Wilson would win, so we didn't bother with too much research into Edward Heath's background. I, of course, was sympathetic to his interest in the arts, and was uncomfortably aware that Harold Wilson showed no interest in any of the arts at all as far as I could tell. Transport House, too, had been wholly philistine. I also strongly approved of Heath's support for closer links with Europe. As polling day drew near, all the commentators and all the polls predicted another Labour victory.

On polling day, I voted very early and then drove through brilliant sunshine to Horse Guards Parade where I parked the car. I went into No. 10 through the Garden Gate. Everyone was there. Excited greetings were exchanged. Already a crowd was collecting in Downing Street. Cheers greeted everyone going in or out. Janet and I bought smoked salmon sandwiches and wine for a celebration lunch. But by the afternoon we knew that our clever, patriotic, kind Prime Minister was out and that Edward Heath was in. While we ate our sandwiches the furniture removal vans arrived.

There was no time to mourn. The phones were ringing

– when was the Prime Minister going to the Palace? We already knew the short drive had been delayed because the Queen would not be back from the races at Ascot until late afternoon. It was after six when the staff lined the stairs and corridor to applaud Harold Wilson as he left for the Palace. The front door closed. Outside, a huge crowd cheered, clapped and wept. It was the biggest political upset for many years. From behind the curtains in Joe's office, we watched in tears.

CHAPTER SIXTEEN

Less than an hour after Mr Wilson's departure, Mr Heath walked up Downing Street through jubilant crowds. Somehow the hundreds outside had rearranged themselves into Tories. We waited with dismay. He looked just like his photographs: sleek and glossy. We turned to the television as he spoke – 'To govern is to serve.' The crowd roared and he moved towards the door of No. 10. Suddenly there were shouts. He half stumbled and, as we crowded into the corridor and watched, our new Prime Minister was bundled indoors, his hair on end, his suit spattered with red paint.

I felt a wave of compassion. He seemed a vulnerable man. This was his greatest moment and it had been ruined. Once again the phones start to ring. Yes, I said, I can confirm that the Prime Minister is here at No. 10. We learnt later that earlier on someone in the crowd outside Central Office had stubbed a cigarette out on his neck. Was he unlucky as well as vulnerable? I wondered.

The first appointment of immediate concern to Janet and me was that Donald Maitland, who had been at the Foreign Office, was to replace Joe Haines. We viewed the appointment of a Foreign Office man with suspicion, a feeling that grew when he told us he wanted our press office to be like the best in Whitehall. 'And which would they be?' I asked. 'The Foreign Office and the Home Office,' he replied. They never say ANYTHING, I thought, but I kept this thought to myself.

The other major appointment at No. 10 was the replacement of the principal private secretary. Sandy Isserlis, who had only been appointed a few weeks before, was replaced by Robert Armstrong. Now all the private office staff were Oxford men, like Heath.

While Janet privately was deeply Labour, she had spent years as an utterly impartial civil servant trusted by all. I, on the other hand, had actually worked at Labour Party HQ, and I was sure the Tories would certainly not want me there with the PM. My view was confirmed by a diary item in the *Daily Telegraph* about my background. I wrote a formal letter to Donald Maitland about my political past and offered to move at once to another department.

Meanwhile, the day-to-day business of the press

department continued, but with a huge difference. Donald was not a tall man, certainly not more than five and a half feet, but he had a commanding presence, and his briefings with the Lobby were almost scholarly. In answer to a question from a tabloid journalist, he might begin, 'As you will remember...', and then summarise the chief points leading to the current policy, while the journalists eagerly recorded this useful background. I learnt as much from the daily briefings as the press did and it helped hugely when answering evening calls. He was witty, too, and a great mimic. There was always a degree of formality in his manner but he was a brilliant press secretary and the press respected and trusted him.

*   *   *

Any formality in the press office was disrupted for ever when, on 6 September 1970, the Palestine Liberation Organization (PLO) hijacked three passenger jets bound for New York. The pilots were forced to land at Dawson's Field, a remote airstrip in Jordan. On the same day, there was an attempted hijack aboard El Al 219. Israeli guards overpowered the two Palestinian perpetrators, killing one in the struggle and subduing the other, a woman. She was flown to London and handed over to the police. Her name was Leila Khaled, a heroine and role model to Palestinian rebels.

A huge international crisis followed. Several hundred hostages were taken by the PLO and threatened with death unless Leila Khaled was freed. While legal arguments were being urgently debated, the world's press focused on London, the Foreign Office and No. 10, particularly after another plane, this time a British VC10 flying from Bahrain, was taken three weeks later and also forced to land at Dawson's Field.

During this period, like the legendary wartime Windmill Theatre, the press office never closed. Doris made tea all night; we took turns in buying sandwiches and fruit. We slept in armchairs. The international crisis was very dangerous. Passengers from many countries were held prisoner, and every country had its own agenda. The Swiss Red Cross acted as mediators, and while diplomats negotiated the media became impatient. Every few days we had to contradict headlines such as 'Leila Khaled Freed!' that came over the wire service. Donald Maitland and Douglas Hurd, who had replaced Labour's Marcia Williams as political secretary, were both ex-Foreign Office so liaison between the departments was smooth and fast.

Finally, at the end of September, Leila Khaled was deported and three planes were blown up by the hijackers after all the passengers were released unharmed.

There was a significant personal outcome for me. Donald Maitland called me in and said that the PM was willing to have me if I wanted to stay.

A short while after the election, the Prime Minister decided to hold a celebration in the State rooms. This would be his personal party, at his own expense, but Janet and I were asked to attend to help with looking after the guests. We were allowed to bring a guest, too, and I invited Edward Greenfield, the music critic of *The Guardian*. 'How lovely!' said Ted. 'I know Heath well. Don't forget I was in the Lobby before I moved over to music.'

At the party, I did my duty for the first two hours, telling guests about the State rooms. Janet and I were informed guides and could talk at length about Sir John Soane, the architect, and about the pictures and carpets. I was watching, full of Labour prejudice, as our Tory Prime Minister talked and joked with his guests when, to my alarm, Ted Greenfield took my arm. 'Come along, Barbara, you said you've not yet met the PM.'

We were introduced. 'You're with Donald in the press office? Good.' He then continued a conversation he had been having with Claus Moser, head of the statistical office. 'It has marvellous sound quality,' he said, 'let's go up to the flat and hear it. You come too,' he gestured to Ted and me. Leave your own party, I thought; how could he! He could; and, getting rid of my cigarette, I found myself for the first time in the PM's flat, desperately trying to decide if the music he was playing was Mozart or Haydn. I listened to their enthusiastic discussion and felt very ignorant. Soon, one of the private secretaries appeared and we were led back to the party.

I told Janet about it the next day. She had been up there often in Harold Wilson's day. 'I expect it's changed a lot,' she said. I hadn't had time to look around much; I was too stunned. It was like being captured by the enemy. There were some very nice pictures on the walls – French, I think.

Soon after that, Ted Greenfield phoned me. 'Are you going to Chequers?'

'What?'

'The PM's holding a musical evening. Isaac Stern, Eugene Istomin, Leonard Rose. Great event, and I can bring a guest. You invited me to No. 10 so I'll take you to this.' This was clearly going to be a grand occasion, so I thought I'd better ask Donald what he thought about my attending.

'Well, it's his private party, but if you're going with a guest…' His voice trailed off.

'Perhaps I should mention it to Robert?'

I went round to the private office. 'Are you interested in music then, Barbara?' Robert Armstrong asked. I said I loved music, although I was not very well informed about it. 'Well, the more you hear the better. I see no reason why you shouldn't go.'

And it was just as the glittering musical evening approached that the catastrophic hijacking crisis had begun.

With doomed airliners in the desert and urgent talks being conducted around the world, I suspected that the concert would be postponed, but Ted Greenfield, his evening dress immaculate, turned up to call for me at No. 10 at the appointed time. I had Doris's map and instructions on how to get to Chequers, and left Janet at the office battling with Leila Khaled.

This was my first visit to the Prime Minister's country house. Security as we approached was unobtrusive – a quick check – and we motored slowly up the drive, my Mini feeling even smaller than it was among the shining limousines in the car park. The Great Hall was full of guests from the arts, but the only one I recognised was the cartoonist and author Sir Osbert Lancaster. This was the first of Edward Heath's musical evenings, which he was to hold at Chequers and No. 10 but, true to what I was beginning to perceive as his permanent bad luck, he wasn't there. He was at No. 10 while planes and their passengers were being held hostage in the desert.

Ted introduced me to several of the guests and then to Isaac Stern. Maestro, I said, copying my escort. The world-famous violinist said he was an old friend of Mr Heath's, and it was a damn shame he couldn't be there. When he then introduced the concert, he called for a moment of prayer for the hundreds of passengers held hostage, and for Israel. The music was beautiful. It was a very special evening. I felt proud and privileged to have been there and wished that our Labour Prime Minister had had a taste for such events.

*   *   *

Life at No. 10 resumed its familiar routine. Janet and I took turns in accompanying the Prime Minister on official visits. At civic luncheons and dinners across the land, when he was the guest, the final flourish for an ambitious chef was a replica of his yacht, *Morning Cloud*, modelled in icing sugar. Everyone knew of his love of sailing and of his racing success. The PM always expressed surprise and pleasure as if for the first time, and the local dignitaries were left proud and pleased.

On one occasion I went with him to Boosey & Hawkes, the music publishers, to see their historic wooden and metal printing blocks and engraved plates of work by Richard Strauss and Benjamin Britten. Most unusually, the driver took us to the wrong entrance. We waited for ten minutes – no welcoming party. Mr Heath was just about to explode when we saw three worried young men rushing to unlock the glass doors. 'Oh, there you are, Prime Minister … welcome, sir … we are so sorry, we rather expected you at the main entrance … come this way … we have been so looking forward to this visit…' The words tumbled out in a flood of relief. Champagne was waiting and the storm clouds receded. Forty years later, at a luncheon party in Suffolk, I met one of the young men who had been on the other side of that glass door. He had been equally apprehensive of a rocket from his boss.

The most important aim of the new Prime Minister was to take the country into the European Economic Community, which later became the European Union. I was, of course, delighted with this policy. All my life I had very consciously felt European. As a child I practised my French on the fishermen from Brittany in Newlyn harbour. When I was working in Mpanda I loved the European mix of British, French, Italian and Austrian. It was then that I first felt that there is a European personality which is quite different from, say, Australian or American.

Although the office knew of my enthusiasm for our government's European policy, I was still unprepared when Donald called me in and asked me to draft a speech on the subject for the PM to deliver. 'You're supposed to know about the arts and Europe. See what you can do,' he said. 'About 4,000 words. Not policy, of course. Send it to Douglas Hurd.'

'Can I go home to write it?'

'Go wherever you like.' He could see how excited I was and laughed. 'Have a go and bring it in on Friday.'

That gave me two days. I rushed back to the press office

and told Janet, who was as surprised as I was. This was not a usual part of our duties. Doris was not impressed. 'They'll probably not use it,' she said.

I drove home, my head full of paintings, opera and books. I found a copy of musicologist Percy Scholes's writings, and looked up Berlioz and his love of Shakespeare. Then I wrote my speech which, inevitably I suppose, reflected my own love of Europe and the arts.

Two days later, my draft typed and retyped, I took it to Douglas Hurd. We had met a few times since the election but had never had a conversation. He made only some minor alterations and was immensely courteous and encouraging. I was almost shaking with diffidence by the time we were summoned to the PM's room. We stood behind him, one on each side, as he slowly read. By the time he had finished the third page without comment my confidence was rising. Then, jabbing at the middle of page four, 'I don't feel this … I don't believe this … Why did you say this?' Oh dear, I thought. Douglas murmured something about deleting. The PM finished reading. 'Well, that's all right. Thank you, Press. Douglas, would you stay behind?

That was my first working meeting with Edward Heath. He had smiled quite warmly I thought, and I had now drafted a speech for a Prime Minister! A few weeks later I was called up to the PM's office again. This time Timothy Kitson and Michael Woolf were there as well as Douglas.

They were discussing a speech to be delivered at the annual luncheon of the Newspaper Publishers Association. The Prime Minister wished to chide the press on their instant reactions to announcements. 'What do you think you're doing here?' Mr Heath was addressing me.

'Listening, Prime Minister.'

'I can see by your face you haven't agreed with a word I've said.'

'Yes, Prime Minister.'

'Well, speak up!' he almost shouted.

I've been bullied by bigger men than him, I thought; Nye Bevan for a start, Len Williams...

'May I have some more sherry?' The men around him looked apprehensive. Mr Heath laughed. 'Fill your glass and tell me what you think.'

From that day on I had a good relationship with Edward Heath. I began to understand his deep patriotism and his earnest desire for closer ties with Europe to prevent another war like the one in which he had fought with distinction. Against all the evidence, he seemed to believe in the essential reasonableness of humanity, and he hoped that by bringing the TUC and the CBI in for talks with the Cabinet, our huge economic problems could be solved. Above all, I admired his courage as the economic weather worsened.

After this discussion in Mr Heath's room, I felt much

more confident about undertaking a draft speech for him. The audience included all regional and local newspapers in the UK, and the PM wanted to talk to them about instant reactions to government announcements. He felt that perhaps not enough considered thought was given to in-depth coverage, although he knew that in a highly competitive industry there had to be swift responses.

I drafted a reasoned speech which was amended and approved by his advisers and, to my surprise, they left the final paragraph alone. I knew the lunch would be generous, and that by the time Mr Heath rose to speak, the editors would be relaxing with coffee and brandy. I thought I'd wake them up with the speech's ending: 'And so, gentlemen, I have one final request. If I can't have a higher level of analysis, may I please ask for a higher level of abuse?'

He sat down to a storm of laughter and applause. I loved that moment, and was thrilled when he thanked me on the way back to No. 10.

It was not long after this that I was asked to accompany Mr Heath to Bonn for the day. He was to make a speech to mark the anniversary of a very pro-Europe speech that Churchill had given there just after the war. Some days before we left, I was called to the private office by a Foreign Office man who was concerned with protocol.

'When you accompany the PM, you must always walk fast, unless he's stopped to talk to someone; don't talk to any strangers, there are always people who try to become friendly. And you will wear a hat, won't you?'

I didn't even own a hat, so off I rushed to John Lewis. I was going to wear a black suit with a white blouse, and there in London's trusty department store I saw the hat. Black and white with a very wide brim – almost a sombrero.

All went well as we flew into Bonn. After the speech there was a reception, and then the PM, Robert Armstrong and I were shepherded swiftly into the back seat of a large, sleek black limousine. We slowly drove away past cheering crowds who had come to catch a glimpse of the British Prime Minister but, unfortunately my large-brimmed 'sombrero' largely obscured him from view. I was deeply embarrassed when I realised this.

'I'm so very sorry about the hat, Prime Minister,' I apologised when we reached the airport. 'The Foreign Office told me I had to wear one.'

'I do not think it was really necessary,' he decreed gravely, and as I turned away I heard them laughing.

While political and economic crises kept us busy all day and most evenings, ordinary life moved on. In October 1970, President Nixon flew into the UK for lunch at Chequers. When the President of the United States comes to lunch, every job, however humble, is important, and Mr Nixon was not the only guest that day. The Queen was going to Chequers, too. My responsibility was to look after the photographers at Heathrow. Security was intense. There were special passes for certain areas. I was festooned with passes. As soon as the motorcade left, I was able to relax and return to No. 10.

When the action moved to Chequers, one of the policemen told me later that there were three lots of armed security present: Her Majesty's, the President's and the Prime Minister's – all watching each other in the grounds.

As Christmas approached, I was asked to choose the prime ministerial Christmas card. I was proud and pleased to be trusted with the task but soon realised that everyone else was engaged on much more important work. I was told to look at Mr Heath's collection of minor French Impressionists – an enjoyable diversion – and I suggested a work by Antoine Léon Piée. The painting featured an elegant young lady on a wooden pier, looking through binoculars at some storm-tossed sailing boats. Her dress of grey-green silk was the height of fashion in 1900. The boats, clearly caught in a strong wind, are leaning at a perilous angle, yet her hair is immaculate! It was Mr Heath's first official Christmas card from No. 10.

CHAPTER SEVENTEEN

The driving ambition of Edward Heath's political life was to achieve closer ties with Europe. His vision for the future was a Europe without wars. During 1970 and 1971, one of Mr Heath's main preoccupations was to gain entry into the European Economic Community (EEC). He visited most European capitals, holding talks on various economic problems, from New Zealand dairy farming to the West Indian sugar industry, with the Common Agricultural Policy (CAP) always the main bone of contention. These talks culminated in face-to-face negotiations with President Pompidou in Paris in May 1971; nearly a year after Mr Heath came to power. To the surprise of many in our contingent, they developed a genuine rapport.

In Paris, the regular press group who followed the PM around was joined by dozens of journalists and photographers from all over Europe and the Common-wealth. The negotiations took place in the Rue du Faubourg Saint-Honoré, where the British Embassy was convenient-ly situated next door to the Élysée Palace. The talks lasted for two days and there were many rumours to be denied as they went on. Donald Maitland, chief British spokesman, was masterly in explaining the complex negotiations to the waiting media. At the end of the first day President Pom-pidou gave a grand dinner at the Élysée Palace. The next day our highly regarded, almost god-like ambassador, Sir Christopher Soames, held a memorable lunch at which the hugely distinguished guest list was headed by the French President, a signal honour in protocol terms.

My job on this occasion was to look after the pho-tographers who were covering the arrival of guests. The journalists clamoured unsuccessfully for details of the menu, since it was well known that Sir Christopher's chef and his wine cellar were the envy of every French hostess.

Guests began arriving in the embassy courtyard. Valéry Giscard d'Estaing, then the French finance minister, re-jected a limousine and walked through the courtyard. 'I don't know what he does for you, Barb, but he sure as hell turns me on,' said a strapping and unusually uninhibited Australian male journalist with a grin of pleasure, as the politician with a film-star face strode past us.

At the end of two long days, the final press conference

was held at the Salon des Fêtes. In this grand room in the Élysée Palace, the chandeliers were even bigger than those in our embassy. As the Treaty of Rome was initialled, many of the British press were clearly moved. They had followed this story for years. I recall that both Nora Beloff and Hella Pick, two of Britain's most distinguished foreign correspondents, had tears in their eyes. I certainly did. I knew I was very fortunate to be present when history was being made, and I felt very proud of our Prime Minister and what he had achieved.

I did not see the formal signing of this world-changing Treaty in Brussels in January 1972. Once again, Edward Heath was unable to enjoy one of the great moments of his life. It was a hugely important day for him, and an historic day for the UK and the European Economic Community, but as he arrived at the ceremony, a young German woman threw ink all over him. She was protesting, not about the EEC, but about her financial investment in the redevelopment of Covent Garden. The signing was delayed while Presidents and Prime Ministers waited for Mr Heath to be cleaned up. Timothy Kitson, his parliamentary secretary, described Heath as looking like someone from one of those minstrel shows. His face and neck were black and it took an hour before he was presentable. I again thought him a truly unlucky man.

By this time the press office knew many personal – indeed, intimate – details of the Prime Minister's life. We were asked questions about the oddest things – his shoe size, how many hours of sleep he needed, where his grandparents were born. Here, we were helped by that biography drawn up by the Royal Society of Genealogists. It was interesting to compare Edward Heath's family history with that of Harold Wilson. Where Mr Heath's antecedents are lost with his great-grandparents, Mr Wilson's go back for many generations of Yorkshire fathers and sons.

The PM loved conducting musical performances, which he had begun while an organ scholar at Balliol, and regularly conducted the annual Christmas carol concert at Broadstairs, his parliamentary constituency. While economic crises rocked the government, Mr Heath still found time for musical events. He was especially delighted when, in November 1971, André Previn invited him to conduct a concert with the London Symphony Orchestra at the Festival Hall during their centenary celebrations. It was an intensely happy moment for him. 'To conduct a great orchestra was the fulfilment of a long-standing fantasy,' wrote his biographer, John Campbell, though I think Mr Heath would have described it as a dream and an ambition rather than a fantasy. He chose Elgar's 'Cockaigne', a very English piece that resonated with his proud patriotism.

The press wanted to take rehearsal photographs at the Festival Hall the day before the concert. When the PM was working informally he had taken to wearing an old, shapeless cardigan, which emphasised his expanding waistline. Always concerned about his public image, I wondered if I dared risk his wrath by saying something to him. I decided I must. I knew he had someone who shopped for his clothes so I hoped for the best.

'There is one thing, Prime Minister. Are you going to wear that cardigan?'

'Why ever not? It's a rehearsal.'

'Well, it is rather old. A new, more tailored one would look so much better, don't you think?' He grunted. When the photographers arrived for the rehearsal he was looking fine: smiling, excited and wearing a very smart new cardigan with shoulder pads.

On the night, the Festival Hall was packed and the music critics were out in full force. I knew most of them, and I knew they would not be kind if they disliked Mr Heath's interpretation of the music. Happily, they were very appreciative, with Joan Chissell in *The Times* going so far as to welcome the debut of a new conductor: 'We could well hear more of this Mr Edward Heath.'

Those final months of 1971 were happy days for the Prime Minister, despite the difficulties bedevilling the government over the economy, the trades unions and the media. He had achieved a lifetime and internationally significant ambition by taking Britain into the EEC, and he had successfully conducted a world-famous orchestra.

The economic climate, however, became even colder in the following year. The media, and indeed most of the Tory Party, blamed their Conservative Prime Minister. I occasionally heard, or overheard, discussions from which it seemed that Mr Heath, patriot and idealist, really seemed to believe that it might be possible to work with the Trades Union Congress for the good of the country. Having watched and heard our trades union leaders across the table at Transport House, I knew there was not a chance that they would co-operate.

Throughout 1972, ministers, trades union leaders and academic advisers trooped, tight-lipped, in and out of No. 10. Controls on wages and prices were introduced and oil prices went up. In an attempt to counter hostile comments in the media, Donald Maitland suggested open briefings after Cabinet meetings. The Lobby members were out-raged. They were proud of their status as intermediaries between No. 10 and their newsrooms. They would not be bypassed. The idea was dropped.

CHAPTER EIGHTEEN

In September 1972 I was honoured and excited to accompany the Prime Minister and Robert Armstrong to the Olympic Games in Munich. We flew to Munich early enough to watch the end of the pentathlon. We were only five rows above the track to see Mary Peters flash past to win her gold. The PM was one of the first to congratulate her, so there were some good pictures of him for the media.

That evening I accompanied Mr Heath to the opera house for a performance of Britten's *Gloriana*. Doris had told me that when a civil servant was instructed to wear evening dress, he was given a clothes allowance. I checked with Estabs but my request was refused; the rule did not apply to women. I wore a long, sleeveless black dress and my best earrings and the Prime Minister sported an immaculate white evening jacket. We sat in a VIP box looking down on millions of pounds' worth of dazzling jewellery. The opera was received with tremendous enthusiasm. It was a wonderful production, beautifully sung, and I went to bed feeling so proud of our British composers, singers and athletes.

The next morning, 5 September, I hurried down to breakfast and was surprised to find Donald Maitland there, deep in discussion with the PM, their expressions grim. Palestinian terrorists, calling themselves the Black September group, had broken into the Olympic Village, killed two Israeli athletes and taken nine others hostage. I learnt that after negotiations between the German government and the Palestinians, it was agreed to fly the terrorists and their hostages to Cairo. In preparation for this they were all taken to the NATO air base.

Meanwhile, despite this quite shocking news, we had a morning party to host at the stadium, even though the day's Games had been cancelled. It was a melancholy occasion. All the British team were there. Cakes and beverages were served, a few token photographs taken. The media wanted to be where the action was, which was no longer at the stadium. After sombre handshakes and good wishes, we left. In the car Donald told me that we were flying to visit Willy Brandt, the German Chancellor.

We drove to a military base and I found myself in a German army helicopter flying over the Scharnsee. Mr

Heath was on his way for talks with Chancellor Brandt at Germany's equivalent of Chequers.

When we landed I was able to shake the handsome Mr Brandt's hand before the group moved off. I sat in a little grey waiting room and drank coffee and felt pleased that I had worn my highest heels. The Chancellor's glance had been comprehensive, but I was uncomfortably aware that I was just a bit of the PM's luggage which couldn't be left behind.

Their meeting concluded. Donald gave me the further appalling news that all nine Israeli athletes had been shot and killed in a brutal massacre at the NATO air base. Five of the terrorists were dead and the remaining three had been captured. Altogether, eleven athletes died, but the remaining terrorists were held captive for only a brief time. A month later a Lufthansa passenger jet was hijacked and there were threatening demands for their release. The German government, under extreme duress, complied and they were let go.

We did not return to Munich, but flew to Kiel where the yachting Olympics were to be held. At our hotel I walked straight into a party where I saw the friendly face of the *Times* journalist, Dan van der Vat.

'What are you doing here?' I asked. 'All the media are in Munich where the action is.'

'At *The Times* we have an old-fashioned notion that we should be where the Prime Minister is,' he replied.

Dan told me that there would be a commemoration ceremony next day at the waterfront for the murdered Israeli athletes. Would the Prime Minister be there? Yes he would. Of course he would.

I then saw Tom Bridges, our Foreign Office man from the No. 10 private office. I told him of my conversation with Dan. 'Why did you say that? That is quite wrong,' he remonstrated. 'The Prime Minister is very tired. Tomorrow he is going sailing on *Morning Cloud.*'

'I don't think so,' I said, and then I caught sight of Mr Heath. 'Why don't we ask him?'

I explained to the PM that he didn't have to speak; he just needed to be present alongside other national representatives and be in the pictures which would be taken. 'There will certainly be a picture on the front of the *Mail* if you are not there.'

The prime ministerial response, as we would have expected, was, 'Of course. *Morning Cloud* will have to wait, I'm afraid.'

We returned to London later that day.

* * *

The next assignment for me was to organise a party. The Prime Minister had, early on, expressed a wish to clean up London – literally. Scrubbing away the grime from

London's public buildings was difficult and expensive. Often the soot and dirt of hundreds of years was the only thing that kept ancient monuments standing, so there was as much expense in cleaning as in making good. The project required some of both, but by the autumn of 1972 Whitehall and central London were gleaming white and the PM wanted to celebrate the achievement.

I planned a guest list with the help of former colleagues at the Department of the Environment, plus adding names of appropriate guests whom I knew Mr Heath would like to be present. I sent a note of these to the private office and got back a scribbled message: 'Good. Now write excellent short speech.' No one had ever given me such flattery. At last I really felt as though I could think of myself as a writer.

Mr Heath's major shortcoming as far as his staff were concerned was his temper. Sometimes he seemed unable to control his sudden outbursts of angry impatience when displeased.

On the night of the party, I was helping to welcome the flow of guests to the State rooms. Most had arrived when I heard the PM's voice, ominously loud, from the corridor. I went to investigate and found him red-faced with rage, shouting at an embarrassed Robert Armstrong. 'I don't care where he is or what time it is. I want him now!'

Robert fled downstairs and I, inwardly quaking, handed the PM a copy of his short speech and told him that most of his guests had arrived. I had no idea why he was angry but hoped he would calm down rapidly – which, thankfully, he did.

The PM left the room and one of his private secretaries explained that Mr Heath had had to walk across Parliament Square instead of being driven in his official car because of an apparently immovable traffic jam. He had then insisted on phoning Desmond Plummer, leader of the Greater London Council, to complain about the capital's traffic flow, despite the fact that Plummer was away in Tokyo, and fast asleep!

True to form, ten minutes later, after his phone call, a smiling Prime Minister appeared, and delivered his speech with perfect aplomb.

Among the occasions when my planning wasn't quite as foolproof as it should have been, was during a visit to New York to attend the celebrations of the twenty-fifth anniversary of the United Nations. It was my first visit to this great city and I was overwhelmed by everything. Again, as in Dar es Salaam all those years ago, I felt as if I were walking into a very glossy Hollywood film. We had a whole floor – a very high-up floor – of the Hilton Hotel, with a glass-fronted chute for carrying mail next to the lift, where I watched fascinated as a river of letters cascaded down. Security was very tight, and I had a New York cop, straight from the movies, outside my door all night. He was big and heavy and festooned with equipment, including a frightening gun and nightstick.

The next morning, I accompanied the Prime Minister to the glorious United Nations building. I felt a glow of pride at seeing the Barbara Hepworth sculpture by the entrance. Her studio was in St Ives, and we proud Cornishmen and women thought of her as one of our own, even though she was actually born and raised a Yorkshirewoman. As Mr Heath walked around, greeting dignitaries in the great concourse outside the conference hall, a very senior BBC interviewer stopped me.

'Do you think the Prime Minister would do a short interview – why he's here, what he expects to get out of it? Fairly general stuff.'

The PM agreed and we arranged to meet in half-an-hour's time. The round conference hall is encircled by a wide corridor, around which the PM and the BBC man strolled, chatting, while I walked behind. Every few minutes some politician would stop Mr Heath to welcome him and shake his hand. Gradually, we walked a complete circle of the hall and ended up where we began. 'We'd better get on with this interview,' the PM said, and both men looked expectantly at me.

'But where is the BBC studio?' I asked.

The broadcaster stared at me in dismay. 'I don't know. I assumed you'd have booked one.'

'Well, I'm going to get a coffee while you two sort it out,' said a clearly exasperated PM, and marched off.

The BBC man sighed. 'We'll just have to postpone it,' he said, and walked away. Feeling an absolute idiot and very nervous of the PM's wrath, I caught up with him. As he did from time to time, he surprised me with his reaction.

'Don't worry, Barbara. Absolutely typical of the BBC.' Later on, when I was on the board of an ITV company, I remembered Mr Heath's comment with pleasure, but the incident certainly wasn't at all typical of the highly professional BBC.

During the quiet days just before Christmas, someone from the press Lobby rang to ask if we had any seasonal stories for them: important Christmas cards, or... his voice trailed off as he lost inspiration. I promised to have a think and ring him back. Donald Maitland then told us that the Prime Minister had flown to Belfast to visit our troops. We were not to say a word about this until he was actually seen there. We waited impatiently until at last the phone rang. It was John Cole, the BBC's Northern Ireland correspondent.

'Barbara, we've just had a flash that the Prime Minister has been seen on the walls of Derry. You're going to deny it, aren't you?'

'No, John, he's there to visit the troops.'

'Oh my God!' John rang off.

I rang the journalist who had wanted something, anything, for a story. Would the Prime Minister on the walls of Derry do? It was a big story, and both we and the journalists were busy for the rest of the day.

Early in 1972, Janet Hewlett-Davies left No. 10 on promotion. She was to return with Mr Wilson after he won the 1974 election and continue her highly successful career, heading the information divisions of two major Whitehall departments before retiring from the civil service.

Not long after Janet's departure, I heard that there was a vacancy for a principal information officer in my old department. I was torn between staying at No. 10, which I loved, and the lure of possible promotion. To my surprise, I really liked Edward Heath. Not only did I share his love of the arts and his commitment to Europe, but I also admired his patriotism, obvious sincerity and hard work. But principal jobs did not come up very often, so, after more difficult and private deliberation, I applied for the position.

I left No. 10 in a shower of good wishes from everyone from Donald Maitland to the policemen on the door. Doris warned me sternly to 'Take care where you're going, with all those ministers falling over each other.'

It felt strange to be back in a more hierarchical set-up. The experience of working at No. 10 had increased my confidence a great deal. For the first time I had worked with highly educated, highly intelligent people who treated me as an equal – or at least allowed me that illusion. They trusted my judgement and encouraged me to contribute, and they ignored my junior rank. Now, despite my new title and status, the more senior members of the civil service with whom I worked once more made it quite clear that my rank was still junior to theirs.

Happily, this did not last long. To my great surprise I was summoned to an interview in the Cabinet Office by somebody from Estabs. He explained that a new ministerial position had been created, that of minister responsible for government communications. A private secretary to the minister was required.

So, in 1973, I returned to sandwiches for lunch and parking on Horse Guards Parade.

CHAPTER NINETEEN

The minister in this new post, to co-ordinate government communications, was Geoffrey Johnson Smith MP, a former journalist with ITN. He, of course, had the final say on whether I should have the position. I met him, we had a good discussion about government publicity, and it was clear that we could get on well together. With his background, he had excellent news sense and I had by then been in the civil service for long enough, seven years, to know my way around the corridors of power – literally, as well as metaphorically, since the Cabinet Office was in Downing Street, and I wouldn't be too distant from Mr Heath after all!

Mr Johnson Smith did press me on one point during the interview. 'You must admit, Barbara, that the civil service is pretty left-wing really, isn't it?' He knew, of course, that I had previously worked at Transport House, but his reference to this was quite unusual and I threw caution to the wind and remonstrated with him. I said how, in most cases, one had no idea of the private political views of one's colleagues; that ever since I joined the civil service, I had been impressed with how information officers and private secretaries worked so unsparingly for whomever democracy had voted into power. I quoted a principal information officer in MinTech, ex-army, who was extremely right-wing, anti-union, anti-Semitic, a horror. His minister was Tony Benn and he worked flat out for him. It was not only quite possible, but also quite usual, to be objective at work.

As this was a new post, we had to create a routine. Geoffrey and I spent much time in No. 10, borrowing the key from the Cabinet Secretary's office to go to and fro. Every Friday morning we met chief information officers from all Whitehall departments. They would inform us of announcements and White Papers in the pipeline. Our meetings were a useful forum for all of us, particularly when policies overlapped departments, or when there was the chance of two big announcements clashing on the same day.

In the afternoon I would compile a list of 'Forthcoming Attractions' and at the end of Friday we would go to the office of whichever Cabinet minister was responsible for Information. I loved these discussions at the end of the week. Geoffrey was a popular young politician, and we were always warmly welcomed. I fondly remember when William Whitelaw was the responsible minister. His greeting was so warm and friendly you would have thought he hadn't a care in the world. We drank whisky and went over the publicity hazards of the week ahead, as far as we could predict them. He was a very wise, experienced and insightful politician.

Sometimes, after Geoffrey had left for his constituency, there might be a phone call from ITN or the BBC asking for help in finding an MP for a weekend news programme. Politicians are not always in a rush to defend unpopular policies, but sometimes I could suggest a backbencher who might welcome the chance of a national broadcast.

The three-day week was beginning to bite by now. Rubbish was piled high in Trafalgar Square. There was a grey feeling of gloom everywhere. The media announced bad news with menacing headlines. No. 10 wanted, as usual, to find out what the public really felt, and how much they really understood the government's policies. Geoffrey and I were called over to No. 10 to meet someone from a market research company. This was the first time I had encountered attitudinal research. The researcher was an American, Liz Nelson, who founded Taylor Nelson, a highly respected listed company. Liz, who has never stopped inventing new ways of market research, lives in London, and we have been friends ever since.

At this time, the government was also worried about the news stories coming back to the UK from British journalists based in Brussels. It was felt that it would help if a minister could go to Brussels and give them a private briefing on the government's policies. Geoffrey Johnson Smith, with me alongside, was chosen to meet them and conduct what Donald Maitland called a 'tour d'horizon', with emphasis on our troubles at home. Until I met Donald Maitland, I had not realised how French our formal diplomatic language is. I particularly liked *dementie*: a denial.

Before our visit I prepared background papers on the main topics we wished to discuss, based on material from the relevant departments. Brussels was awash with British ambassadors – one for Belgium, one to the EU and one to NATO. We were to stay with Sir Alan Beith, the Ambassador to Belgium.

We flew Queen's Flight, as usual, from Northolt, Geoffrey as eager for a few days away as I was. We were met by an official car and taken to the ambassador's residence, a lovely old house in a wide, tree-lined road. Lady Beith welcomed us, and announced that they were in the happy position of having two butlers. 'They are gay and will only work together, so I took them both,' she said. 'They are invaluable.'

I was surprised by her liberal views. 'Our Foreign Office people are often like that,' Geoffrey told me. 'They respect convention when they have to but they are quite sophisticated, too.'

Our meeting with the journalists was to be held in private after a dinner at which their wives were present. There were no women journalists in the pack. It was a formal dinner with some twenty people seated at the long table, beautifully set, where we enjoyed an excellent meal.

Just before coffee was served, our hostess stood up and looked around the table with a significant and commanding expression. The wives then stood, too, and Lady Beith gave me a stare until I found myself also standing up. As we filed out of the dining room and the door closed, I heard Sir Alan say, 'Come along, gentlemen, move up this way … Geoffrey, you sit here … let's get down to work, shall we?'

I turned to Lady Beith as we moved into a large sitting room laid with coffee cups and drinks. 'I'm sorry, Lady Beith, but I must go back to the dining room.'

'You can't possibly, my dear. The ladies always leave; it's convention.'

'But I'm Geoffrey's private secretary. I've done all the work on this.'

'Well, you must do what you must, I suppose, my dear, but it will be the talk of Brussels among the ladies tomorrow.'

Lady Beith looked upset, and I felt sorry about that, but it not only seemed idiotic not to be there for the discussion, but who would take a note? Once again the administration was slow to recognise that women were also now senior civil servants. I went back along the corridor and slipped into the dining room.

'Ah, there you are!' Geoffrey greeted me with evident relief.

'Madame, vous prenez du café?' It was one of the butlers. 'Oui, merci, et un cognac, s'il vous plaît.'

'Gentlemen,' announced Geoffrey. 'This is my private secretary, Barbara Hosking. We can begin now.'

I had no idea whether there was any gossip in Brussels about my staying with the men, but I certainly hoped so. I enjoyed, as I always did, the feeling of being something of a trailblazer, even if I was once again exceeding my brief. Sometimes our great institutions were, and sometimes still are, very slow to learn that the day of the woman was, and is, coming. Fast.

CHAPTER TWENTY

Throughout this time, the political weather worsened. Mr Heath tried in vain for some sort of consensus. The heavy feet of trades union leaders seemed to echo constantly throughout the house. I knew them, and knew there was no hope of compromise on any of the issues when, in their view, they had the government on the run. By 1974 it was clear that there would have to be another general election. Everyone seemed to be against the Prime Minister, including his own party: the right-wing Enoch Powell urged his fellow Tories to vote Labour.

Left with little choice, on 28 February 1974, Mr Heath went to the country with the slogan, 'Who Governs Britain?' This time it was no surprise when, on that same date, Harold Wilson returned to 10 Downing Street in triumph.

While Geoffrey Johnson Smith had been away

campaigning in his constituency ('There are no safe seats now, Barbara'), I stayed on in the Cabinet Office with little to do, relishing long lunch hours and short afternoons. I also had time to go out with friends, do some cooking and catch up with opera-going.

After the election results had been declared, Janet Hewlett-Davies and Joe Haines came back to run the press office. It was decided to keep the ministerial post for co-ordinating government information and Labour's John Grant MP, a former industrial correspondent, was appointed. He was not obliged to reappoint me, but after we'd talked about people we both knew, he decided to keep me on. John was thin with wispy, fair hair, rather a loner and very keen on keeping fit. His wife acted as his secretary, although in practice he had the sort of London constituency where there was little correspondence and the local party sorted out any problems. He was conscientious about his weekly constituency surgeries, and had led a quiet political life. As a junior minister he was anxious to co-operate with Joe Haines on all policies; where I would argue, he deferred. His background was similar to Joe's, and they were both impatient with what they perceived as middle-class tastes. John, for example, genuinely felt there was more virtue in eating fish and chips, with a pint of beer, than a grilled herring and a glass of plonk, though they cost the same.

He loved being a minister, although he thought red boxes were old-fashioned. 'Do we really have to put up with this rigmarole?' he asked me.

'These boxes are very secure – they are lined in steel – and your work is confidential,' I explained.

'Well, you've turned into a model civil servant,' he teased, knowing my political background. 'Tell me, Barbara, the civil service really is totally Tory, isn't it?'

'No, it's not,' I protested emphatically, once again having to explain to a minister that almost all civil servants kept their political opinions to themselves and worked conscientiously for whomever the voters chose. John Grant obviously didn't believe a word of what I said.

Mr Wilson sometimes assigned John to events where, unusually, a ministerial presence was necessary. This was why, when there was to be a UN conference on population in Bucharest, he suddenly found himself designated Minister for Population.

I had never been to Romania and looked forward to the possibility of accompanying John. 'I will only take you if you bring your bathing suit with you. I must keep up my swimming,' he said. I happily agreed that swimming was part of my private secretary's duties, and off we went in August 1974.

We were booked into the Athenée Palace Hotel, famous as the place of the notorious assignations between ex-King

Carol II and his mistress, the mysterious Madame Lupescu. The rooms were heavily decorated with thick velvet curtains and still evoked a sense of cloak-and-dagger drama. This feeling was emphasised when our Romanian minder, a pretty young woman with excellent English, refused to join us in John's suite to discuss our plans. We had always to join her in the lobby.

At the conference the delegates listened to the speeches in translation through their headphones. My best moment came when, after a long, impassioned speech by the Vatican representative, there was a robust response from a delegate who pointed out that the Vatican was the only place on earth with no population problem of any sort!

The conference concluded with Romania's annual celebration of freedom from the Fascist yoke. The country had changed sides in 1944, in time to emerge on the winning side – just as they had done in 1918. We were invited to see the parade, and were very surprised by the absence of any spectators other than the President and his top brass. The people watched on television, we were told. Such was communist security.

We stood beside the viewing stand, next to high-ranking army officers in glittering uniforms and highly polished boots while, above us, President Ceaușescu and his generals took the salute. I love the precision of marching men; after all, I am my father's daughter. John heartily disapproved and was glad when we could leave. That evening we had supper in a leafy square where the food, the wine and the square itself could have been in a Parisian quartier. What a delightful and puzzling contrast to where we had been earlier.

The next day, John wanted to go swimming. The Romanians wanted us to see more of their country. Both desires were met. We were taken to Count Dracula's castle to swim in his lake. The Count's popular name was Vlad the Impaler, and I was told that the lake was where his victims finally ended up. It was a hot day, the water was clear and cold, and I swam with pleasure until I strayed near the edge of the lake. Weeds quickly circled my legs and, stupidly, I froze in fear. After I had swallowed a mouthful of lake, I forced myself to swim, spluttering, to the steps, my towel and safety. In the sunshine I watched while John swam lengths for an hour. On the way back to London he teased me about my swimming – 'You didn't do much, did you, Barbara?' I refrained from telling him why.

In 1976, when I was still in the Cabinet Office, there was a small but amusing disturbance in the corridors of power. Peter Hennessy, a particularly good Lobby journalist with the *Financial Times*, could always be relied on for accurate, perceptive comment. Suddenly, he appeared in *The Times* with the by-line 'Whitehall Correspondent'. Uproar among the mandarins: What the hell does *The Times* think it's doing? How dare they? Whitehall Correspondent indeed! What a liberty; what an intrusion! The mandarins were definitely not happy and an instruction was issued not to give Hennessy any separate briefings, and certainly not to accept any lunches! The ban did not last long. We needed his important pen.

Not long after this, I learnt that there was a vacancy coming up for a senior position at Environment. I loved my work in the Cabinet Office but opportunities for promotion didn't arrive very often. I applied, was shortlisted, interviewed, and appointed chief information officer at the Department of the Environment.

Once again, it was farewell Horse Guards Parade and hello Marsham Street.

CHAPTER
TWENTY-ONE

It felt very odd to be back in the brutal Environment building. However, despite its unattractive home, the department was the first ever government ministry in the world founded to deal with environmental matters. It was an umbrella department, covering everything from birds and bees to oceans, farms, roads, rail, aviation and the property services agency. Remarkably, we had twelve ministers: the Secretary of State, three Ministers of State and eight junior ministers, each of whom, ostensibly, had a little empire to run. It was helpful to the Prime Minister to have so many politicians with their eager feet on the first rung of the ministerial ladder, and one of my unspoken responsibilities was to find them things to do. It was popular with everyone if they could be invited away to open something.

The information department at DoE was equally big. My boss, Neville Taylor, was the Director of Information. He looked after the Secretary of State and ran the information division, helped by two chiefs – Roy Long, who was responsible for paid publicity, films, posters and booklets; and me. I looked after the media, with the help of a dozen press officers – one for each minister. I very much enjoyed being responsible for so many staff and tried to be a good boss, office door open and always available to listen and support. Naturally, I liked some of them more than others, but I tried not to show it.

I got on well with Neville, who was a wise, tolerant ex-journalist. He had a calming influence on ministers, who sometimes worried about the reaction of No. 10 to their speeches and were always worried about the reactions of the media. He had a calming effect on me, too.

It took me some time to slow down after the daily adrenalin of Downing Street, where news followed news like waves crashing on the cliffs at Land's End. As work slowed down to a less demanding pace, my leisure time increased and I had more money to enjoy it. I bought some lovely clothes and went to theatres and the opera more often. And there was also more time for my friends, for whom I cooked enthusiastically from the recipes of the immortal Elizabeth David.

It was, in a way, reassuring to go back to the never-ending

saga of the third London airport, still ongoing. In 1971, the year before I had first arrived to work at the DoE, the government had announced its final decision on the site. It would be built on mud flats to be reclaimed at Maplin Sands in Essex. It was a huge project, envisaged to include a high-speed rail link to London, a deep-water harbour for container ships and a new town of some half a million people.

There were endless planning inquiries which, to our surprise, were especially loved by the middle classes who could, for the first time in their lives, legitimately experience the wicked pleasure of carrying a banner and disrupting a meeting. It reached its apotheosis for me when the headmaster of Winchester sat down in the middle of a main road, singing, 'We shall not be moved!' in a demonstration against the M3 bypass.

I had one press officer whose full-time job for a while was to deal with publicity generated by an energetic group of bird lovers. They were worried about the fate of some rare geese that lived on dwarf eelgrass, which grew exclusively at Maplin. With the return of a Labour government and an oil crisis, the Maplin Sands solution was abandoned and the rare geese continue to eat undisturbed.

As summer drew on, Neville and Roy, both family men, went on holiday along with most of the department. I have never liked the long summer break that Parliament allows itself. It is a hangover from an earlier, pastoral England, but one could hardly expect our tradition-heavy Parliament to change, so London empties as the temperature generally rises. That summer of 1976, the temperature rose and rose and continued to rise. As the land dried up and water disappeared, my department had to issue emergency regulations banning the use of hosepipes. My limited staff were inundated with calls from the media about tales of horticulturalists going bankrupt, flocks of chicken slaughtered and fires breaking out.

There was a division within the department which looked after all government buildings at home and our embassies abroad. It was headed by a most senior civil servant, Sir Something-Something. Given the continuing water shortage, I was startled when one of my press officers came to me with some strange information. 'I've just been told that we are going to wash and clean the front of 1 Victoria Street.'

'Are you sure this isn't a joke?'

'No. I know it sounds mad but it's true, and they're going to begin next week.'

I phoned Sir Something-Something's private secretary and he confirmed this, explaining that they had committed to an expensive contract. 'I'd better speak to Sir Something-Something,' I said.

I was put through. 'To whom am I speaking?'

'Barbara Hosking.'

'I don't think we have met?' He didn't sound friendly.

'I am a chief information officer and the most senior press officer here at the moment. I understand that there is a contract to clean the facade of 1 Victoria Street?'

'That is correct.'

'But, of course, it will be postponed now, won't it? We have forbidden the use of hosepipes, businesses are failing—'

'I don't think you understand the cost of this contract,' he cut in. 'This is government money.' Sir Something-Something was now very unfriendly.

'And I don't think you understand public reactions. Perhaps you would like me to invite the media to send some cameras?'

'Nevertheless, the work will go ahead,' he said, and with that he put down the phone.

For a moment I was at a loss. Everyone was away. Should I go up and see this man? No, I didn't think that would help. I decided there was only one person who could stop this. I rang my old friends, the switchboard at No. 10, and asked to have a quick word with Robert Armstrong.

I explained the problem to Robert, who laughed. 'Well, he's certainly looking after the pennies. Don't worry, Barbara; I'll have a word with him. Thank you for letting me know.'

Late that afternoon, Sir Something-Something's private

secretary rang me. 'We've stood down the cleaners. Come up and have a drink, the coast is clear. I didn't know you had worked at No. 10.' When retired government information officers meet for enjoyable reminiscences in old-fashioned London wine bars, this is one of the stories I most enjoy telling.

The major problem at that time was the great rivalry between road and rail. Each fought for money, for ministerial attention and for public support, and it seemed to me that road always won. If I were writing a weighty account of the great policy clashes of the '70s, road and rail would occupy many chapters, but what I like to remember are the small but valuable achievements during the drought, when my colleagues and I had to be brave and speak truth to power.

PART IV

FIGHTING MY CORNER

CHAPTER
TWENTY-TWO

As my fiftieth birthday drew near in 1976, I had to make an uncomfortable decision. Ten years stretched ahead before I would reach the compulsory civil service retirement age. I had progressed from the lowly rank of assistant information officer to chief information officer. I had helped to tell the world about laser beams and hovercraft. I had watched the arrival of two Prime Ministers from the windows of 10 Downing Street. I had had my own grand space in the Cabinet Office as private secretary to a minister. What in the next ten years could compare with the thrill of working at the centre of government? I had been a very small cog in a very large machine, sometimes working twenty-four hours a day, but I had been a very happy cog, totally fulfilled in playing my part. The civil service had been very good to me. At its best, there was an invigorating pragmatism and I had been encouraged to take responsibility, make decisions and speak up. Now, at the Department of the Environment, my work followed a predictable routine as White Paper after White Paper was followed by press conference after press conference. There was more time for planning and publicity for ministerial visits at home and abroad. If I stayed at Environment there would be uninterrupted evenings and weekends and possibly one more promotion. If I were to move, now was the time.

Just as when I had first come to London from Cornwall to seek my fortune, I looked in the newspaper for vacancies; not in the *Evening Standard* this time, but *The Times*. It didn't occur to me to ask any of my colleagues for advice, and my friends had little knowledge of my sort of work.

As soon as I read the advertisement for a director of information at the IBA, I knew it was the job for me, and, so certain was I that it would be mine, I didn't even bother to apply for anything else. After all, I reasoned, I had often accompanied government ministers to television interviews and had broadcast several times on Radio 4 myself. My daily bread-and-butter work was talking to journalists, including radio and television journalists. Of course, like any ordinary television viewer, I knew nothing about regulation; in fact, I hadn't a clue whether the programme I had liked last week had come from ITV or the BBC. Regulation, I decided, was a matter of counting swearwords.

Fortunately, pride on this occasion did not come before a fall, and I was invited to interview for the post. Two preliminary interviews were easy, but then I was told that the third and final one would be with the full authority, rather like the interviews when I was on the Islington Council. I looked up the members of the Authority in *Who's Who* and planned my responses to any questions I thought they were likely to ask. The authority comprised twelve distinguished members, including a physicist, an ex-politician, an educationalist, a trades unionist and other representative figures. It was the usual mixed bag put together by a conscientious government and therefore, of course, included two women and one ethnic minority person.

I decided that, if I possibly could, I would mention my press release on lasers. That would interest the physicist, while some references to Transport House and Nye Bevan would interest the trades unionist. I tried to arm myself with something for each of them, just in case. I was also asked to provide an example of my published work, and chose a piece from the *New Scientist* where I had written about copulating crabs in a television programme.

I knew with all my heart that this job was meant for me and I enjoyed the final interview. What I did not know when I was offered the post was that I would have a company car and an expense account, and I certainly did not know there would be media interest in my appointment. According to one newspaper, I had achieved the top publicity job in London, while another wrote of the 'grey hand of the civil service' falling on independent broadcasting.

In early March 1977, before starting my new job, I took two weeks off. I had been given a most generous farewell party at Environment and there were thank-you letters to write. I celebrated with Robin and Ann and gave two dinner parties at home. I have kept a hospitality diary since 1965, the only diary I have kept, and I can see how my cooking and entertaining improved from pizza and Blue Nun in the '60s. Soufflé and good claret now made regular appearances. I also spent many hours getting to know my Audi 80. I had moved from Islington to be near Robin, finally taking an apartment in the beautiful block of flats in Crouch End where she and Ann lived. Robin was very keen for me to move nearer to where she lived with Ann. I was delighted. My commitment to her was deep and permanent. Ann may not have been overwhelmed to have me as a neighbour but there were compensations for her, not least borrowing my car, and we had many close friends in common. I happily moved from Islington to Crouch End. It was open plan, with my own garden in front and a large communal garden at the back where we had parties in the summer. The building had its own car park, so no more looking for space in the evenings.

The only real sadness as I started my new career was the death of my dear elder sister Peggy. I knew she had been ill, but she seemed to be perfectly well. She died suddenly of a heart attack just as our grandfather had done. I had loved my brilliant, temperamental big sister very much, although after I left home I didn't see her very often. As I sat with our sister Sheila at Peggy's funeral in Landrake church, I thought fondly about how she had defended me at school when I was teased about my arm, and how she had encouraged me when I went to the Isles of Scilly. I remembered, too, how she had bought a beautiful camel-hair travelling coat especially for the twenty-minute flight from St Just airport to St Mary's. That was so typical of Peggy. Once again I wished that I had made more time for my family.

On Monday 28 March 1977, I took possession of my beautiful office at the IBA overlooking Harrods. The first task I carried out that morning was to hang two photographs on the wall, one of Harold Wilson and one of Edward Heath, both signed and inscribed with warm messages of thanks for my work. I needed their support! I also arranged some beautiful roses that had been sent by Gillian Reynolds of the *Daily Telegraph* with a message of congratulation. It was my first contact with one of the media journalists, and I wondered if she had any inkling of how frightened I felt and how grateful I was for her welcome. Over the years we have become firm friends. Gillian is clever and funny, adult and wise. She is also the doyenne of broadcasting journalists, with a deep knowledge of the history of broadcasting. Who needs Google when they can ring Gillian?

My office was as big and luxurious as my previous quarters in the Cabinet Office, but it was very different in style. I now had several low tables, a sofa and armchairs – and a refrigerator: the tools of the trade. From here I could brief a group of journalists over drinks or lunch. From my windows I could see the proud 'By Appointment' insignia which in 1977 graced the facade of Harrods. I thought of the years of sandwiches eaten at my desk. I had certainly not imagined that the change would be so great.

My deputy was John Guinery, an Oxford graduate and former London editor of a regional newspaper. I only discovered later on that he felt cheated of a job that he had expected would be his.

I was fortunate in my secretary, a serious young woman with a degree from Edinburgh and a lovely smile, who spent some of her free time at Holy Trinity, Brompton, the nearby church where Alpha courses first began. She told me that young people at the church made themselves responsible for lonely old people and kept an eye on them. I had done no volunteering for many years and resolved to do better. Anthea was loyal and would always go the second mile, although I felt that she rather disapproved of the amount of wine that was consumed in my office.

On my first day I arranged for all the information division to come to my office so that I could meet them in person. There were some fifty of them. I asked John Guinery to introduce them to me, but he refused. Sadly, this was the first shot fired in a silent war not of my making.

CHAPTER
TWENTY-THREE

George Cunningham had been right. I had thrived in the civil service and it had given me the experience and confidence to compete for a top position. My life was going to be very different. Not only the Audi and the salary, but in future I would be the boss, and I would have to give my best advice directly to the director general, Sir Brian Young. Fortunately, he was charming and courteous, and was quick to put me at ease. He had an impressive academic background and had served in the Royal Navy during the Second World War. My one link with my old life was my parliamentary pass. I would be expected to keep up my relations with politicians, especially those involved in education and broadcasting and, accordingly, I came to act as an informal conduit for information between the IBA, MPs and the media.

In the '70s, broadcasting was always in the news. ITV and commercial radio competed fiercely with the press for advertising revenue, so if a programme ventured too far into realism, the 'delicate sensibilities' of newspaper editors could be outraged. Newspapers, when they choose, can be 'easily shocked', and this can quickly infect politicians; questions could be asked in the House. Life, as I very soon learnt, was never quiet at the IBA, even before the redoubtable Mrs Mary Whitehouse rallied her supporters to safeguard the morals of the nation.

The very concept of regulation might seem odd to many people – if they know it exists. For example, if an actor goes too far in a comedy, viewers might be shocked but they rarely complain (especially not nowadays), and usually the incident is immediately forgotten. But occasionally, during my time, audiences were genuinely shocked, or felt – as they still do – that a news programme was unfairly biased. The IBA was then swift to act, conducting an investigation and, if merited, issuing an apology.

As the regulatory brief included monitoring sex, violence and vulgarity across all programmes, there was plenty to keep us busy. Drama often provoked tense and heated discussions; the rape scene in *The Forsyte Saga* was a prime example. But it was not only plays, drama series and comedies that we had to watch over. Television news editors often worried over what to include in footage of warfare and disaster; how much horror to show remains a very real question for broadcasters.

Advertising was a separate and very important division. Every claim made in a commercial had to be proved true – so no miracle cures were peddled on ITV! I had to learn all this very quickly because the most important task at the IBA was the reallocation of television broadcasting licences for the different regions, when existing TV companies had to reapply for their licences against bids from competing newcomers. There was strong competition for these licences which, if not a licence to print money as they were once described, were nevertheless extremely profitable.

I had been recruited two years ahead of this crucial and lengthy process, during which the existing companies were assessed and those judged to have underperformed lost their licence to a newcomer. The great strength of ITV when I was there was that it was regional. The companies varied in size from Granada in the north with its millions of viewers to little Channel Islands TV, which still flourishes today when all the rest have gone. Major regional companies competed to produce the best news, drama and documentaries, and their programmes provoked the BBC into improving its output, too.

Many look back at this time as a sort of Golden Age of

television. ITV drove standards up and we all benefited. It is often assumed that the BBC introduced regular religious broadcasting, but it was ITV; and it was ITV who first introduced coverage of Parliament. *Brideshead Revisited* and *The Jewel in the Crown* were Granada's, and *The Darling Buds of May* was made by Yorkshire Television (YTV), both companies which hardly exist nationally today, although their regional news is still first class.

My job was busy, challenging, exciting. The only shadow was that my deputy, John Guinery, never really accepted that I was the director. We achieved a working relationship somehow, but it was too much to bear when, checking the annual expenditure for my division for the first time, I discovered that his salary was higher than mine. I suppose I had assumed that a quango would have the same rules on equal pay as the civil service; instead, I had gone back to a system that discriminated against women financially. I checked with our finance director. With some embarrassment, he confirmed that no, it wasn't a mistake.

I was furious. It was the first time I had experienced real unfairness at work since my early days in Wardour Street when women had to clock in with the boys. I charged down the corridor to Sir Brian's office, shot past his surprised secretary and barged into his room. His attempt at calming me down didn't help.

'After all, he has been here longer than you,' he said.

'Does your deputy get paid more than you?' I shot back, and explained that it just wasn't fair. Sir Brian was a former housemaster at Eton and headmaster of Charterhouse, so his knowledge of working women was probably not overly extensive, but the appeal for fair play evidently struck a chord.

'I will see that the situation is remedied today,' he said, after listening carefully to my argument.

At the end of the afternoon, the finance director rang through with details of my new salary. He called me a suffragette in an admiring tone, and said we now had two suffragettes in the company, the other being Lady Plowden, our chairwoman.

I had only met the chairwoman briefly since my appointment. She was tall and slim, with a powerful presence and the assured diction and command of the English upper class. Tiresomely, I still found it difficult not to defer to an aristocratic voice. As I watched Lady Plowden work and interact with Sir Brian, I grew to respect and admire her. Her Christian name was Bridget and her friends called her Biddy, but I learnt that her second name was Horatia and that she was a niece of the intrepid explorer Gertrude Bell. Powerful genes there.

As the date for licence renewal drew nearer, Lady Plowden quietly let it be known that she would not consider any application that did not have provision for women both on the board and in senior executive posts. I was delighted to pass this on in answer to requests for advice on applications. Some ITV companies grumbled, but they all complied. We often quoted, with delight, one company chairman who during his formal interview explained, 'But Biddy, I have nothing against women as such.'

I met an amazing range of interesting and impressive people in this new life where work and leisure merged, and some of these became friends who would have a great impact on my life. One such was Ian Coulter, a former journalist who had become director of information at British Steel. I met him when I was asked to join a group of directors of PR in nationalised industries and quangos who lunched regularly in each other's boardrooms. Ian was a member of the Reform Club, and when that club voted to accept women into membership in 1981 he invited me to join. I have been a member ever since and have served on the committee. It is a most beautiful building, with a fine library, and the membership is diverse and fascinating. It plays a big and happy part in my life.

My meeting with Mary Baker was even more important. She was a powerful player: first woman on the board of Barclays Bank, a director of Thames Television and chairwoman of the London Tourist Board. I first met her at the IBA when we were celebrating a Thames Television win in the Prix Italia. She was interested to see what this new woman, who had emerged from the anonymity of Whitehall and been written about in the *Telegraph*, was like. We became friends immediately, and have remained firmly so ever since. I love Mary Baker's Scottish wit and admire her sharp business brain.

When I was elected to the Reform Club I decided I would go there on my own for lunch. I was so nervous that I went by mistake into the Travellers Club, where I was politely, but firmly, shown the door. As soon as I went into our beautiful saloon, I met friends and political journalists who, in those days, lunched at the club after their morning briefing at No. 10. I resolved to show the members that they had made a prudent choice in electing me to membership: I invited Edward Heath to join me for lunch there. 'What a lark!' he said. 'Not my usual haunt.'

When he walked into the saloon it caused quite a stir. 'Hello, Ted, what are you doing here?' more than one surprised member asked.

'I'm having lunch with Barbara Hosking.'

'Who?'

I had made my mark. Mr Heath ordered lemon sole, which he said was sweeter than Dover sole, and we talked politics and people and how music was doing in London. It was kind of him to accept my invitation, and gave me standing in the club from the start. Later, I invited Harold Wilson and Marcia Williams. By that time, sadly, his mind often wandered away during conversation. After Harold's appearance at my table, I was promptly elected to the political committee, the senior committee which went back to the founding of the club.

The Reform Club had opened its heart to me and I worked hard to repay this honour.

CHAPTER
TWENTY-FOUR

Three years after I joined the IBA, we were due to announce a new franchise round. Excitement had been building for many months because the current ITV companies had held their broadcasting licences for many years without challenge. The introduction of colour television had imposed a heavy financial burden on the ITV companies and it was considered unfair to ask them to incur all the expense of a reapplication as well. In addition, a ten-week industrial dispute in 1979 had cost them an estimated £100 million in lost revenue – as well as public anger at the absence of *Coronation Street* during that time.

It was therefore a dramatic moment when, on 28 December 1980, Lady Plowden announced a new franchise round. She also announced the introduction of an additional franchise: breakfast television.

ITV was regional or it was nothing, and the IBA was determined to extend this regionalism. Already each broadcasting company had its own newsroom and journalists, but this was to be extended to even more regional coverage by breaking up the current news coverage into smaller geographical areas. Our gifted TV engineers enjoyed the challenge of making this work, and small, state-of-the-art news studios opened up across the country. Throughout the 1980s, UK viewers enjoyed this professional news service focused on their own areas.

Having announced the composition of the new licences, Lady Plowden's time in office ended. I had greatly enjoyed working with and for her. She came from a distinguished line of men and women who have served this country well, and had added her own contribution with warmth and integrity. She greeted our occasional failures with a sympathetic 'most discouraging', and our triumphs with a confident 'most encouraging'. She left an important legacy in her quiet, strong support for women.

Lady Plowden's successor was very different. George Thomson had been a Labour MP for twenty years. He had had an important political career as a moderating influence on the Labour Party, and as an enthusiastic supporter of Europe he was one of the first European commissioners.

He came to us as Lord Thomson of Monifieth, Knight of the Thistle, and asked us to call him George. He was a Scot, a former journalist who started as a trainee with DC Thomson, editing *The Dandy*. He was delighted that I had once worked at Transport House, and when we were away from London we would sometimes reminisce about the Gaitskell battles.

The other big change was the appointment of a new director general to succeed Sir Brian Young. Sir Brian had all the authority of a public school headmaster; indeed, 'headmaster' was his nickname at some of the ITV companies. He had been scrupulously even-handed in his dealings with our licence holders and they respected him and his decisions. His successor was really chosen by George Thomson, although the post was advertised and there were two strong internal candidates. It was clear that the government wanted a change of style and they certainly got it when George named John Whitney, the founder and first managing director of Capital Radio, as the new director general. John was a charming, buccaneering, commercial radio hero, and in his own account of his time at the IBA, *To Serve the People*, it is clear that he was urged to apply for a position he would never have otherwise considered.

It was an extraordinary change for me, too. After the measured tones of Sir Brian, to whom the black arts of publicity did not strongly appeal, I was now faced with a streetwise populariser who, at his first management meeting, ticked off one of my colleagues for using a Latin quotation. He had begun that meeting by taking off his gold Rolex and standing it on the table in front of him. This may have been how commercial radio conducted its meetings, but it was certainly new to us. It was a difficult beginning, though, for John Whitney. His two immediate lieutenants, the heads of television and radio, had been passed over for his job, and their Oxbridge superiority and outrage were not always well concealed.

The internal politics of any organisation are often complicated, but now I had a new ally. The new deputy-chairman was Sir George Russell, a sociable ex-businessman who liked to drop into my office at close of play to talk broadcasting and politics. I thoroughly enjoyed his views on events, often so different from mine, and we shared a huge love of music. Although he was a very successful businessman, George and his wife enjoyed an unpretentious lifestyle. They had brought up their children in a comfortable family house in Hampstead, and still live there today.

It was the new guard at the IBA who, in 1982, made the final decisions on the broadcasting licences. Two contractors, Southern TV and Westward TV, lost their licences. Two years later, Channel 4 was launched under the experienced command of Jeremy Isaacs. It had unusual parentage in that it was owned by the IBA and fully funded by the

ITV companies – no licensing necessary – who supplied Channel 4's advertising and took the profits from it. Channel 4 is still independent, although now it raises its own revenue and is government-owned. I do wonder how long it will be before the financial predators pounce. After all, for many in the City, it is intolerable to see a not-for-profit business thriving with no shareholders and no dividends.

This was an especially busy time for the information department, with two new broadcasting channels preparing to launch. Breakfast television attracted most of the media attention because Peter Jay, the son-in-law of former Prime Minister James Callaghan, was running it with the help of celebrities, including Angela Rippon, David Frost, Anna Ford and other media stars. They built new studios by the canal in Camden Town, decorating the facade with egg cups.

I had met Peter Jay from time to time over the years, and now he rang me to request help with publicity. He couldn't, or wouldn't, understand why I issued information about Channel 4 but refused to do the same for him. I explained that TV-am, the title of breakfast television, was an independent business with its own licence to broadcast, while Channel 4 was actually owned by the IBA. He would have to employ his own staff.

'You just like Jeremy [Isaacs] more than me,' he complained ruefully, though whether in jest I couldn't tell.

However, I did want to help poor Peter if I could, since he simply never seemed to understand the rules and he did need someone to publicise TV-am's launch. I remembered a very bright young woman on my staff at Environment, Tanya Ossack, who had left the civil service early to have her first child and qualify as a barrister. I rang her and explained the problem. We discussed the fee and agreed that the salary she had earned when she was in Whitehall would be fair. How innocent we were! A professional publicist would have charged five times more. Tanya did excellent work for her starry employers and the channel took off for a tempestuous future.

Their first problem was the BBC. As soon as Lady Plowden had announced a breakfast service, the BBC began planning to open a similar programme and launched their service two weeks before TV-am. To add to Peter Jay's problems, they opened with a lightweight American-style magazine format. This was desperately hard on Peter and his team. They had planned a highbrow style for his 'mission to explain', as he described the philosophy of the station. Clearly, TV-am had very quickly to go down-market or they would have no viewers. No viewers, no income. In addition, there had been a failure to agree advertising rates and so the station began with almost no revenue. Within three years Peter's company was replaced by another, headed by Jonathan Aitken MP. The IBA's rules did not allow an

MP to run a television channel, so breakfast TV was run by his cousin Tim Aitken. The station's fortunes did not really improve until Roland Rat arrived. He was a children's puppet and, as someone quipped, it was the first time a rat had joined a sinking ship.

A British initiative to showcase the best of British arts was organised in New York in 1983. This festival, called Britain Salutes New York, was held at the Metropolitan Museum. The International Women's Forum, a nationwide American women's organisation, wrote to Mary Baker at the London Tourist Board to say they were surprised that so few British women were involved in the festival events. They invited her to bring a small group of women to New York for a week, on an official visit. Mary asked me to be one of them, and Sir Brian agreed that I could go, to represent the IBA. That's how I joined Katharine Whitehorn, Oonagh McDonald MP and the High Mistress of St Paul's Girls' School, Heather Brigstocke, among others, and flew across to a warm welcome in New York.

Our hostesses, a group of prominent women who had created the International Women's Forum (IWF), were an inspiring lot who led us on a merry dance from a private breakfast at Tiffany's – yes, really – to a walk in Central Park and a succession of enjoyable lunches and dinners. Many speeches were made, including one I gave about the IBA. It was an exhilarating time. Here I was in New York, travelling with nationally known, highly successful women who welcomed me as an equal. I had admired Katharine's brilliant journalism since she first wrote for *The Spectator*. Heather Brigstocke was a great educator; she was also a most beautiful woman, which brought me to a very odd realisation.

From the time I left the civil service and entered this new life where clever, successful, gorgeous women were becoming my friends, I was never attracted to any of them. I happily led a conventional social life, not hiding my home life wherein women sometimes came and went, but not talking about it either. I assumed that sophisticated people would know I was gay, while the unsophisticated still invited me to spend Christmas with them so that I would not be alone.

On the plane journey back to London, we resolved to form a branch of the International Women's Forum in the UK. I felt it would never happen unless we had some public record of our decision. I rang Roy Hodgson, the editor of 'Men and Matters' – the title given in those misogynistic days to the diary column in the *Financial Times*. I told him of our visit and suggested it might be worth a paragraph.

'Well, you'd better write one,' he said. So I did, and the founding of the first overseas branch of the IWF was duly recorded for posterity.

For some years we remained a private organisation of

some thirty women, no rules and no fees. We met in each other's boardrooms. One of our members was the racing driver and businesswoman Jean Denton, later Baroness Denton and a government minister for Northern Ireland. She felt that we should have a higher profile and a bigger membership. So in 1989, under her leadership, we split into two overlapping groups, with individuals choosing which group was most convenient for them to join. Today, as part of the IWF we have hundreds of members, including permanent secretaries, a former head of MI5, vice-chancellors of universities and CEOs of FTSE 100 companies. Our original little group, now known by the name Links, happily continues with its private dinners, while our thriving sibling provides a great opportunity for women to make friends, network and offer support and encouragement when it becomes tough at the top. In 2016, as part of our twenty-fifth anniversary, the portraits of our founders and chairwomen were painted by members of the Lots Road Group of artists. Together with short biographies, they have been on display in the headquarters of both HSBC and Barclays banks for the edification and, we hope, inspiration of their younger female staff.

CHAPTER
TWENTY-FIVE

My chief task at the IBA was to publicise our work and explain our decisions, using all the range of publicity ammunition at my disposal – and more, when I could! I had spied a golden opportunity to do this early in 1979 when the other Lord Thomson, the owner of *The Times*, closed the paper in an unsuccessful attempt to curb the print unions. I learnt that all *The Times*'s journalists had to report in every week to receive their pay even though they were not working. I contacted the editor and suggested that his staff should spend a day with us. Our various heads of department would explain the reasons for decisions on drama, politics, news and advertising. We would try to make it an enjoyable day. We would give them a generous lunch and tea and try not to overload them with too much dry factual background. As newspapers almost never strike, journalists are never available for such an event, so this was a heaven-sent, one-off opportunity to explain our policies to an important group.

Nearly a hundred journalists turned up and were welcomed by Sir Brian. An unexpected bonus for me was hearing that the BBC was very miffed! My opposite number there, Michael Bunce, was berated for not having thought of the idea first. Michael and I were good friends. We often shared platforms at media conferences and worked together at festivals abroad, so I bought him lunch as consolation.

The two main international television festivals were the Prix Italia for drama and documentaries, held in a different Italian city each year, and the Rose d'Or de Montreux in Switzerland (still the Rose d'Or but no longer at Montreux) for comedy programmes, where the prized Golden Rose, oddly enough – or so it seemed to us – was frequently won by Norwegians. There was always great rivalry between ITV and the BBC, but Michael Bunce and I helped each other with information. However, there was one occasion in Italy when he couldn't help. My chairman, Lord (George) Thomson was invited to a grand BBC dinner for all the television chairmen, which Michael was organising. My chairman had his wife with him, and asked me to see if she might accompany him. I approached Lord (George)

Howard – the joke then was that everyone senior in television was called George – and asked if Lady Thomson could attend with her husband. Yes, she could. However, it appeared that Lady Thomson had an old-fashioned habit of taking a friend abroad with her as a travelling companion. Lord Thomson now asked me to find out if the travelling companion could also come to this dinner. I went back to Lord Howard and asked whether, in these unusual circumstances, perhaps another exception could be made. He replied that, while he was prepared to accept George's wife, he was damned if he would accept his mistress too! Needless to say, I had to find an emollient refusal for Lord Thomson, and reported that 'regretfully' there was simply no more space in the restaurant to accommodate this request.

It was at this time that I was awarded an OBE. It could not have been more unexpected; I certainly wasn't aware of having done something special, and I was certainly not about to retire. I had no idea who nominated me or why, but I was delighted. I bought a new silk suit to wear to the Palace, and took Robin as my guest. By happy coincidence, at the time we were preparing a special day at the IBA when the Queen would be coming to lunch with us. When the Queen asked me what I did, I replied that I did the same job at the IBA as Michael Shea did for her. She was immediately interested and said that she was looking forward to her visit to the IBA. 'So, we will meet again,' she said.

A month later, the senior staff lined up in the hall at the IBA to be presented to Her Majesty before lunch. There were eight of us and I was the last. As Lord Thomson presented each of my colleagues, the Queen smiled and nodded, but said nothing. When she reached me she said, 'I told you we would meet again, and here I am.' Seven pairs of senior eyes swivelled left to glare at me in disbelief as we talked. Once again, it seemed, I had gone too far.

I was now often invited to speak, not only on regulation but also on women's issues. I was active in the 300 Group, a lobbying group formed to increase the number of women in the House of Commons to 300 – a goal which has still not been achieved, but comes ever closer. It was cross-party, and it was then that I saw at first hand the hard work of the Tory women. On several occasions I went to conferences in Cork organised by the poet Maire Bradshaw and her group of committed Irishwomen. They were interested in politics and literature and they were full of energy and enthusiasm. Sometimes, when I stepped off the plane, I was rushed straight away to a radio studio to be interviewed on why I was there and what I thought about some current news story. This was at a time of great violence in the North. My good friend Jean Denton was now in the House of Lords – in fact, I had the pleasure of joining her family to watch her take the oath of allegiance and to share a celebratory lunch afterwards. She was now a junior minister in the Northern Ireland Office and I thought it was about time I told her of my agreeable links with the Republic. I also wanted to sound her out about an idea I had been pondering for a while: to organise a conference in London for women from both sides of the border. I firmly believed, and still do, that there would not be so much violence if women had more power, and I hoped a weekend together might encourage those wives and mothers, sisters and daughters, to work together for a positive future for their beautiful island. Ridiculously grandiose hopes, but Jean listened. She could not help officially, but she gave me the names of some fifteen senior women in Northern Ireland who she felt would accept an invitation. With the help of my friends in Cork, I found fifteen women from the Republic.

Now all I needed was the money. I started with the Bank of Ireland, whom I asked for £5,000, as I did all further donors, to cover all the expenses of air fares, hotels, special dinners etc. Every company I approached, on both sides of the North–South divide, paid up and the money rolled in. Once again I had hit on an idea which seemed to be meant to happen. The Regent Palace Hotel near Piccadilly gave us a favourable rate for the weekend. I went through my address book and assembled the most talented bunch of women I could muster. A date was agreed, return air fares bought, and with finance and a venue, hey presto, I had a conference!

There was a full programme of talks and discussions on women's issues and, of course, on the major topic of peace. On Saturday night we held a dinner in the library at the Reform Club. The speakers included Nancy Seear, Shirley Williams, Julia Neuberger, Heather Brigstocke, Mary Baker and Katharine Whitehorn. The evening ended with the women singing Irish songs. A 'first' for the Reform Club, too.

On Sunday the Protestants went to the service at Westminster Abbey and the Catholics to Westminster Cathedral. Some of the ladies from Cork had brought brothers who were priests, and they assisted with the Mass. There were special prayers for our conference. Afterwards, we had coffee and hot buttered scones made by the nuns, with the Cardinal in his private apartments, before joining the other half of the group for lunch.

I had wondered what to do with the ladies on Monday, but Michael Cocks, a former deputy chairman of the BBC, now Lord Cocks, agreed to host a final morning of discussion, then lunch, at Canary Wharf where he was deputy chairman of the London Docklands Development Corporation. Sunny Crouch, an old friend who ran the British World Trade Centre, arranged this, and provided a splendid farewell meal. When I formally thanked Lord Cocks, I told the conference that he had a fine voice.

'Give us a song!' they shouted. He stroked his tie and sang the beautiful German song 'Du bist wie eine blume' in a pure tenor. Thirty female Irish voices sang back to him, and suddenly we were in danger of missing the plane. Just in time they joined their coach for Stansted.

Many friends had helped with the conference, including some from the 300 Group, and we were thrilled when two of the women who had attended signed the Good Friday Agreement. We hoped that in some small way we might have contributed something towards this peace.

There was another surprise outcome for me later, when I was awarded an honorary doctorate by the University of Ulster. Their chancellor, Rabbi Julia Neuberger, had taken part in the conference, and she and the university felt that it had been important enough to merit this recognition. I was jubilant. A degree at last! You can't use it, of course, my friends told me. That would be too vulgar. I, of course, wanted to flaunt it. I would have worn my beautiful blue hood to Waitrose if I'd thought I could get away with it! In the end, I had to be satisfied with having the letters added after my name in my cheque book.

It was about this time that Robert Armstrong rang me from No. 10 and asked if I would be interested in running the public relations at the Royal Opera House. Among his responsibilities, Robert was secretary to the board. He told me that Sheila Porter, the critic and musicologist, Andrew Porter's sister, was leaving, and he thought I had enough knowledge both of music and publicity to do her job well. I was very tempted. It would be an exciting and glamorous life. My friends were most insistent that I should take the job – then I was told that one of the perks was two stalls seats every evening. No wonder they pushed me! I went to see John Tooley, the general administrator. We discussed what the work would involve, and he asked me about myself and my musical knowledge. He was a pleasant man, and I knew that this was a great opportunity, but I quickly decided that I would not apply. I had been at the IBA for six years. I found the work interesting and sometimes demanding, and I wasn't sure that I could face another complete change of career.

The IBA is a very British compromise. Even the word 'regulate' shows a British style. Far from the censorship of a dictator, but it might be considered illogical to regulate one part of the media – broadcasting – but not the other – newspapers. Freedom of the press is the great cry, and it is generally felt that the law is sufficient protection against excess. If I sometimes shudder at a headline, I remember the words of Tom Stoppard: 'It is the price you pay for the part that matters.'

I am not sure now that I entirely agree. When broadcasting

began, the government was terrified of this new form of communication. Every extension of communication has been seen as a threat to the powerful. From the railways to the penny post, rulers have tried to stop, or at least control, development. So, while newspapers gradually gained total freedom in the name of free speech, the fledgling BBC was firmly controlled. When I was at the IBA, it was very important to tell the public how and why we controlled broadcasters. Much time was spent on conferences, public meetings and surveys of public opinion.

We worked in the overlapping worlds of broadcasting, politics and the press, but my media colleagues then were, I thought, the last of the media mandarins. They could easily have been civil servants – they had similar backgrounds and interests – but my mandarins mixed with show business, politics, drama and sport. Our head of television, Colin Shaw, had joined us from the BBC. His discussions were with, among others, Sir Paul Fox at YTV, also ex-BBC, Michael Grade at London Weekend Television and Sir Denis Forman at Granada, who inspired great TV drama and loved opera. I got to know these powerful men. As a Jew, Michael Grade, who eventually held every major job in broadcasting, was amused that I understood some Yiddish, an inheritance from my bedsit days in Swiss Cottage. I was in awe of Denis Forman. He had been wounded during the Italian campaign in the war and had an artificial foot which hurt when he was tired. *The Jewel in the Crown*, one of the greatest drama series since television began, was made under his aegis. Paul Fox always liked to talk politics, and his company produced some of the best political programmes. The senior broadcasters understood the work of the IBA, even though they did not always like it. Inevitably, they spent much time in the company of their scrutineers and there was always respect, and sometimes friendship, between them.

I met Colin Shaw's wife, Elizabeth, at the Rose d'Or Festival in Montreux. After the festival, we stayed on to go walking in the Italian hills, and the three of us forged a close friendship. I learnt that Colin had had a play produced professionally even before he had graduated from Oxford, where he had acted with the University Dramatic Society, and while he was at the BBC later, he acquired a law degree: a true mandarin. The appointment of John Whitney as director general had disappointed and shocked Colin Shaw and the head of radio, John Thompson. They had not expected someone so very different from Brian Young to be chosen. John Whitney had the kindest nature – he was a cradle Quaker – and had left school at sixteen to make his fortune in the rough new world of commercial radio. He founded Capital Radio and led it to great success. Colin, smarting from his rejection, soon left to regulate another quango.

I had no difficulty in adapting to the new regime. John Whitney clearly needed a lot of support in his first months, and I enjoyed his style. Mandarins hardly ever seemed to notice their pock-marked desks and scruffy chairs, whereas John transformed the director general's office into a cool, beautiful art gallery. He chose a long, honey-coloured table instead of a desk, and brought in modern sculptures and contemporary pictures. He also made a decision not to drink any alcohol while he served as director general. He stuck to his resolve from the day he arrived until the day he left, seven years later.

There were several staff changes at this time and the next licence round was beginning to creep up the calendar. I was fifty-eight, two years off the mandatory retirement age. I had been able to transfer my civil service pension to the IBA and, thanks to our kindly finance director, I had been able to buy back years – whatever that meant. I knew I would have to leave early enough to allow my successor time to get to know the industry before the broadcasting licences were advertised once more. Perhaps I should go now too, I reflected. I made an inventory of my finances and felt sure I could live reasonably well on my pension. I owned my apartment in Crouch End and the IBA would probably allow me to keep my car. In two years I would have my State pension too. I reconciled myself to a simple life of grilled herring, salad and plonk. My friends warned me that I would miss the expensive hospitality of my working life. They laughed disbelievingly when I reminded them that I was a Cornish girl at heart and my tastes were simple. I had a talk with John Whitney, who hoped I wouldn't go just yet but understood my wish to lead an active retirement life while I could.

All my family, with the exception of my sister Sheila, have died young, and I felt I would not live to any great age. I was exhilarated at the prospect before me. Robin and Ann were no longer working and many of my friends had recently retired. I thought of all the things I could do with my days: cinema and theatre matinees, exhibitions, lunch with friends, afternoon walks in Kenwood. 'Free at last,' I said, as I contemplated long weekends in Cornwall.

Anthea, my trusted PA, had returned to Scotland and my new PA was Asifa Vanderman. She was born in London but her ancestors were from the high mountains of northern India and she had inherited from them a fine profile and an independent spirit. She had turned into an invaluable PA and I am still in touch with her some thirty years later, though she now lives in California with her husband and son. I confided in Asifa that I would be leaving fairly soon, that there would be the usual announcement, and then the head hunters, but I was not going to tell anyone for a while.

Asifa brought a message that Sir Paul Fox wanted a

word with me. 'I hear you are leaving,' he began. There was no point in my being annoyed. Paul was always first with the news, although I hoped John Whitney was not going to tell anyone else so soon.

'Nobody knows yet. I've only just decided,' I explained.

'Barbara, you remember Alex Todd?'

'Wasn't he director of communications at Tory Central Office? Didn't he die recently?

'Yes, but when he retired he came to me as our political adviser. So now I want you.'

I was amazed, and said so. I kept a close eye on politics, particularly as it affected broadcasting, but it was many years since I had been closely involved. I protested that I had made lovely plans for my retirement and told him about the grilled herrings and plonk. I was very flattered by the offer, I said, but my mind was made up.

'Now, before you turn this down, Barbara, I really think you should have lunch with our finance director. He will explain our offer in more detail. I don't think you should say no until you've seen him.'

'Paul, I have my whole future organised,' I grumbled, 'but I suppose you're right. I'd better know what I'm rejecting, but I am still amazed.'

He laughed. 'We'll speak again.'

I was genuinely stunned by Paul Fox's phone call. I had not considered any more work of any sort, other than perhaps some voluntary work for which I was still young enough. And, I hoped, at last I could settle down and write. My joke was that I had written for everything at least once, so perhaps I could at last produce a book. In any case, what did a political adviser do? I certainly didn't want to move to Yorkshire. Who could I talk to about this? I pulled myself together. I was flattered that Sir Paul Fox thought that I could replace one of the top political operators in the country. And on reflection, I supposed it might also be good fun to stay in the world of broadcasting...

I decided to wait and see what this offer meant. Meanwhile at the IBA, we were still being battered by Mrs Thatcher and the tabloids about violence on the screen. The Prime Minister was probably the lightest viewer in the country and 90 per cent of our output was wholly blameless, but there are always some who will be shocked and some who will see political bias. In the late autumn that year, we watched in sympathy as the BBC was sued over a *Panorama* programme. In the end, they paid damages for calling some right-wing MPs extremely right-wing.

The head hunters were now busy finding my successor and my secret was out. Some of my colleagues and friends in the industry said nice things about me, and the press were kind. There was great interest in who my successor would be and I was pretty interested, too. I hoped it might be another woman but thought it unlikely. Then came the welcome announcement that the new director of my department would indeed be a woman, AND a former civil servant, Colette Bowe. I didn't know her but was soon told about her impressive CV. She was Liverpool–Irish, a strong woman, and the possessor of no fewer than three university degrees. Later, when I came across her remonstrating with some British journalists at the Prix Italia in Capri, I discovered that she also had a remarkable vocabulary. A docker would have been proud of her. Colette blazed a great trail, going from the IBA to Ofcom, and later being made a DBE.

The IBA had its own momentous decision to make that winter. The government had given us responsibility for the introduction of broadcasting direct from a satellite. A licence had been advertised, applications considered and the first contract for satellite broadcasting was awarded. This opened up a whole new era for radio, television and communications. The age of satellites had begun and I organised my last big press conference.

Paul Fox's finance director had indeed taken me out to lunch. He explained that the contract would include a car, and quoted a salary which surprised me. I would go to Leeds once a month to attend the company's management meeting and I would have a weekly meeting with Paul Fox in London. I would also continue to attend all the party conferences, this time representing YTV.

I immediately abandoned my plans for a simple, leisurely and culturally high-minded future. I loved the excitement of politics and the media, and it would be fascinating to see life from the point of view of a broadcasting company. I wondered if the IBA would let me accept this offer. I asked John Whitney and he could see no reason to refuse me. I reminded him of gamekeepers and poachers, and he laughed and congratulated me. George Thomson had the same reaction, so I discussed my new car with Yorkshire, an Audi 90 this time, and prepared for a really celebratory Christmas to end 1986.

The irony, as I took my last leave from Brompton Road, was that the government had just appointed my former boss at Downing Street, Sir Donald Maitland, as the IBA's new deputy chairman. I would have loved to work with him again.

CHAPTER
TWENTY-SIX

It took me quite a while to get used to my new life. The administrative side of YTV was wonderfully efficient with railway tickets, hotel rooms and everything to do with my car. The company was broadcasting twenty-four hours a day, the only television company in the UK to do so. They used a satellite for night-time broadcasting. It was very successful, and they would have continued if the satellite had not failed after the first six months. But it was a glorious six months.

In Leeds, I liked to hear the programme makers discussing their work, the storylines and the cast. The very varied output covered comedy, politics, news and drama. *Emmerdale* and their regional news programme, *Calendar*, are still going strong today. At times, I was very slow to realise what was going on. When, for example, *The Darling Buds of May* was being made, I couldn't understand why all the men found a reason to go and watch the filming. Then I learnt that the young, talented and amazingly beautiful Welsh actress playing the lead was Catherine Zeta-Jones. YTV loved her, but she soon left them for Hollywood.

In London I had coffee each week with Sir Paul Fox. The YTV offices were in one of my favourite parts of London, near Gray's Inn Fields and opposite Lamb's Conduit Street where the pioneer publisher Persephone lives. I looked forward to these weekly meetings, when Paul told me what the company was doing and I told him what I thought was going on politically. He was always very well informed. YTV covered a thick slice of England, from Yorkshire to Norfolk. There were many MPs representing constituencies across this large area, and they all wanted to be interviewed on *Calendar* or some other political programme. Government always kept a suspicious eye on political content and Paul and I never failed to marvel at the sensitive natures of politicians. Happily, the company had an excellent reputation for its political programmes, as well as for series such as *A Touch of Frost* and documentaries like the ones about the prize-winning Daleswoman Hannah Hauxwell. When the IBA announced the date for the renewal or rejection of broadcasting licences, I had no difficulty in finding MPs from all parties to sign an Early

Day Motion wishing YTV good luck and praising their output.

I gradually grew used to having a life of my own, although loving friends were quick to try and fill my time with good works. Members of Forum suggested various charities which apparently needed my help. After all, they pointed out, you have always said you wanted to do some voluntary work when you retired. So I became president of the Media Society, joint vice-chairman of the National Council for Voluntary Organisations (NCVO), and a trustee of the Charities Aid Foundation. It gave me a positive charge of energy to be contributing to such important work, and once again I acquired a new long-term friend, Usha Prashar. Usha was the chief executive of NCVO and, like me, she knew how to find her way along the corridors of power. She came to this country courtesy of Idi Amin, who expelled the Asians from Uganda, and like so many of those unwilling migrants she thrived in her new country.

Usha explained that one of my responsibilities would be to negotiate staff salaries with the trades unions. The agreements we reached were regarded as a sort of benchmark for the whole of the charity sector. The unions were well aware of this, and so was I, and I did not enjoy these encounters. My thoughts went back to Transport House when, as chair of the staff, I had to negotiate our salaries and was amazed at how grudging the trades union members of the

National Executive were. In my ignorance, I had assumed that our negotiations would be benign occasions. After all, we were all on the same side, weren't we? No, we were not. So I didn't relish the thought of more testosterone-heavy encounters. Now when I read of industrial conflict I feel so sorry for all those caught up, often throughout their working lives, in these old-fashioned ritualistic performances. I suppose it is better than physical force, but not much. In 1945, after the war, the British were involved in creating new industrial structures for Germany. These included trades union representation at board level. Surely such a system would improve working lives here? After all, look how Germany has turned out as a manufacturing power!

I kept up with the various women's groups which I supported. Before I left the IBA, I had invited the 300 Group to spend an afternoon with us to learn about the regulation of independent broadcasting. They had also helped with the Irish conference, so now that I had more time I attended many of their meetings where I discovered that the Tory members worked really hard. It is not surprising that we have now had two female Conservative Prime Ministers, even though the second ran so quickly into serious political trouble. The Tory women worked far harder for political power than any of those in the other political parties. We still do not have 300 women MPs, but we're well into the 200s, as of the June 2017 election.

I also worked with Clean Break to help them raise money to buy new premises. This organisation was set up by two women who had been in prison. They knew from their own experience that many of the female prisoners were not criminals but victims – often from dysfunctional homes, often abused, often homeless. Clean Break works through theatre. When I first met them, their dedicated director, Lucy Perman, was working in extremely primitive conditions. Our small, hard-working board raised many thousands to buy and purpose-build an efficient centre with good performing spaces and supporting accommodation.

I had not, however, anticipated the public reaction when we started building. The neighbours objected forcefully, worried that women who had been in prison would bring their criminal boyfriends around to burgle their houses, hold drunken parties and generally terrorise the neighbourhood. Gradually, we were able to persuade them that their fears were ill-founded, and today Clean Break is a huge success. Hundreds of lost young women have acquired confidence and jobs through working with theatre: behind the scenes, front of house and sometimes on stage, too. New plays are written for them, often stories from their own lives, and their work has been performed to acclaim at the Royal Court, the Soho Theatre and the Arcola before touring the country.

In September 1988, I had suffered another family loss

when my brother, Geoffrey, died. He had had a mixed career since those happy early days on the *Falmouth Packet*. He had married June, a lovely Cornish girl with dark hair and merry eyes. He was not really satisfied with a career in journalism and decided to join the Royal Navy. A few years later, he left the Navy and emigrated with his family to Canada, but, unfortunately, that didn't work out and they were soon back in England. I went to see him when he was ill and, as usual, he made a brave show of optimism. He had such a radiant smile, but I could see he was depressed. Then the worst blow of all arrived as he suddenly became totally deaf. Geoff was a proud man and he truly hated this affliction. He railed against the silence so much that it affected his heart and he died. He was only fifty-nine years old.

June had always been an immensely supportive and loyal wife, but now the children were grown up and she had to learn to survive on her own without her much-loved husband. She surprised me with the many imaginative ways she found to support herself, from organising literary festivals to house-sitting empty mansions. I am really proud of her.

My work with YTV had settled down into a happy routine when Paul Fox dropped another bombshell. He was leaving to return to the BBC as managing director of their television network. I was appalled. I didn't want any changes in my life. But life is change, I reminded myself as Paul departed.

I found that I was to report in future to Clive Leach, the new managing director. He was an able administrator, but not a Fox. In any case, politics were less important now that the company's main preoccupation was with the renewal of the broadcasting licence. This time the rules had changed. Decisions would be made both on the quality of the proposals and the amount of money offered to pay for the licence – in effect, it was a blind auction. The results, when they were announced in 1991, were heartbreaking and ridiculous. To give an example, while YTV only just retained its licence with a huge bid of over £37 million, Central Television was successful with a bid of just £2,000. In my view, the Broadcasting Act marked a shameful episode of political fiddling with a successful industry.

As I became more involved in women's issues, I met Tony Lothian, which was how the aristocratic Marchioness of Lothian liked to be addressed. Her Christian name was Antonella and she was a dashing, dark-haired woman with a black patch over one eye that gave her an improbably unconventional appearance. She had lost an eye through illness when she was young and rejected a glass eye in favour of the patch. It was always easy to find her in a crowd. I first met her when I was asked to buy a ticket for the annual Women of the Year lunch. This event was her brainchild, an opportunity to celebrate outstanding women and to raise large sums of money for the blind.

There were always terrific women of achievement to be honoured, and their speeches were inspiring.

Soon, Tony involved me in planning the lunch and helping with publicity. She worked really hard for the Women of the Year and we honoured many deserving women, but perhaps none more deserving than Valentina Tereshkova, the first woman to travel into space. She and Tony became friends, and, in 1990, I was interested to learn that Valentina was planning an experiment. She wanted to invite a senior British group to Moscow for a week to test whether the Russians could introduce a VIP tourist project. Tony asked me if I would like to join the group. It would be expensive but, luckily, I could afford it, and looked forward eagerly to being part of a visit which would open doors usually firmly closed.

Our party, which Tony named the Moscow Fellowship, included Elizabeth Smith, chairman of the Scottish–Soviet Friendship Society and wife of John Smith, the Labour Party leader; Sir Fitzroy Maclean, the distinguished Scots war hero, diplomat and author; Floella Benjamin, later Baroness Benjamin, and a woman of multiple breathtaking achievements. All the rest were Tony's family, Lothians or Buccleuchs. Thus, we had one duchess, a marquess and marchioness, an earl and countess and four lords and ladies. We were about to launch an aristocrats' invasion of communist Russia!

For anyone interested in international affairs, it was a wonderful time to be in Moscow. Mikhail Gorbachev, then at the height of his power, was trying to reform a sclerotic, bureaucratic government. British media crackled with reports of impassioned debates on the future of this great country. I had been to Russia once before when, for a mere £250, Thomas Cook provided air fares and full accommodation for a week's sightseeing. Then, gigantic, grim-faced men stamped our passports and we were hastily herded into a bus. This time we were met with smiles and roses in the VIP lounge at Moscow airport, and were introduced to our interpreters, one for each of us, and talked about the World Cup and *perestroika*. Our accommodation was in the Academy of Social Sciences. It was rather like staying on a university campus, very comfortable, and quite unlike the bleak hotel I had stayed in on my previous visit. There was a reception in our honour in one of the vast public rooms, before we were taken at midnight to see the changing of the guard at Lenin's Tomb in Red Square. It was one o'clock in the morning when we went to bed, beginning a pattern of late nights and early mornings that went on all week.

In the Kremlin Armoury we saw wondrous works by Fabergé and marvelled at a tiny model of a trans-Siberian train in beautiful detail. The final carriage was a chapel. Sir Fitzroy Maclean elaborated on the guide's words and explained the historical background. In 1944, Sir Fitzroy had worked with the Red Army in Yugoslavia to defeat German troops and had been awarded the Red Star for gallantry. He was treated with huge respect throughout our visit, and was a patient and invaluable guide for us.

Despite arriving late and tripping embarrassedly over Communist Party officials while finding our seats in the dark, a great treat was our visit to the Bolshoi Theatre for a performance of Tchaikovsky's opera *The Queen of Spades*. This is a favourite of mine, and to my great delight, we were taken backstage to meet the leading singers. But what really thrilled me most was the memorable moment when I actually walked across the legendary stage of the Bolshoi.

Our visit to Zagorsk, the resting place of St Sergius and home of the biggest collection of icons in the world, gave us an insight into the increasing power of the Church in Russia since the coming of *perestroika*. We had a long discussion on the revival of religion with the head of the theological college, and learnt that atheist parents were now sending their children to Sunday school. Lady Cecil Cameron asked if many young men were now discovering a vocation for the priesthood. This was translated as 'vacations', so we had a long answer about holidays. After this complicated discussion we went down some shadowy stone steps to visit St Sergius's tomb in the crypt. He was rather like St Francis and had wanted to be buried with the poor, only to end up in an ornate tomb of solid silver which shone amid the shadows. Some old women nearby, shrouded in black, sang holy songs in a minor key. We were each given a large, lighted candle and were directed to follow a long line of worshippers. I saw that as they reached the tomb each worshipper made a deep genuflection. Tony, who was strongly religious, was in front of me and as her turn came she suddenly thrust her candle into my hands and prostrated herself across the tomb. I was left with two candles to hold, just managed not to fall over as I genuflected, and returned to our group with what I considered quite justifiable pride.

In a week of extraordinary sights and experiences, none was more memorable than a visit to Star City, an entirely enclosed town where all the population worked on the exploration of space. We were welcomed by Aleksey Leonov, the first man to walk in space. He greeted Floella Benjamin with 'Hello, Blondie', and gave her special attention from then on.

Because of Valentina, we were exceptionally privileged throughout our visit. We saw the Mir space station before it was sent into space. We met two Japanese cosmonauts and watched their weightlessness training in a huge tank, where they looked like fish in some giant aquarium. We asked them about their problems and they said that the worst was learning Russian. In the Gagarin Museum we saw the thin suits that Yuri and Valentina had worn, and

the scorched iron ball in which they flew and had para-
chuted back to earth. We were silent with wonder.

Later that evening we met up with Valentina, who looked
utterly exhausted. While we had been enjoying the opera, St
Sergius and Star City, she had been supporting Gorbachev
all week at the Soviet Congress as *perestroika* was being debated. She said that the recent meeting between Gorbachev
and Mrs Thatcher had been very significant. It was strange
to be aware that this impassioned debate on a great country's future had been going on around us all the while.

After a final reception and affectionate farewells, we left
Moscow tired, happy and enriched by all we had seen and
learnt. All of us were thrilled to have shared for a week in
the momentous atmosphere of peaceful revolution which
Valentina had revealed to us. Our party's undoubted star
had been Floella, who danced and sang with our Russian hosts and made instant fans of them. In November,
Valentina Tereshkova came to the UK to receive an honorary degree from Edinburgh University, and I had the
honour of entertaining her to tea at the Reform Club.

Later still, Tony Lothian published a double biography
of herself and Valentina, describing their unlikely and
strong friendship. When reading it, I particularly noted
the cosmonaut's prediction: 'There will be apple orchards
on Mars.' She explained the scientific basis for her optimism, and I often recall her words as we watch the Mir

space station turning into a sort of cosmonauts' hotel, and the technological exploration of Mars becoming daily more likely.

I came down to earth with a bump when we returned from Moscow. It had been such an unbelievable experience that the tribulations of ITV seemed trivial in comparison with the upheavals of a vast country fighting for a free future. YTV was no longer as happy as it used to be. It was widely recognised that the company had bid too much to retain its licence, so the inevitable cost-cutting which followed meant cuts in staff. I stayed on for a year but soon realised that I was also a cost which could be cut. Clive Leach was not sorry to part with me, so after a final regretful visit to Leeds, I drove my Audi 90 happily back to London and a totally free life.

I had been a member of the Royal Television Society since I joined the IBA and, in due course, was elected to its council. The RTS was particularly good at supporting new entrants to the industry, so when young people ask me how to get into broadcasting I always suggest a good first step is to join the RTS. There was a time, though, when I really went off them. Just after I joined the council the venue for meetings was changed to the Caledonian Club. I arrived there early one evening for a meeting and met another council member, the great Verity Lambert, founder of Cinema Verity, who died much too young.

We decided to have a drink in the bar. 'Out!' shouted the Scottish barman. 'We dinnae serve women.' I shouted back loud enough for anyone near to hear, 'We are not women. We are Scotchmen in drag.' We were very quickly shown upstairs to our meeting room, and it didn't take us long to work out that our treasurer was a proud member of this Scottish club that did not admit women. The RTS council listened to the angry protests of the women members and our meetings were held in more appropriate surroundings from then on.

I now had time for longer holidays. I went with Robin and Ann to India twice, and to China, where Robin was born. Her mother came from a missionary family and her father had been head of Shell in China. She had a photograph with her, taken when she was a child in the garden of her parents' large house. We found the house, which is now a museum to Chou En-lai. I also went for weeks or long weekends with Links, the women's group I helped to found many years before. We visited most European cities and, memorably, Marrakech, where we worried the Moroccans dreadfully. There were ten of us, and we were constantly asked who was looking after us. It appeared that they had never before seen a group of women travelling independently – not even one man to look after them.

My long weekends with Mary Baker, Katharine White-horn and Heather Brigstocke – always the same four – at

Mary Baker's Spanish retreat were highly prized. We all swam, Mary windsurfed and we ate fresh grilled seafood, washed down with local plonk, at the tiny harbour. Every evening we talked books, music, theatre and politics. One evening during a heated discussion in which Katharine had been talking about homosexuals, without even thinking I said, 'Well, you must all surely know that I am gay.' If I had produced a gun and fired it through the roof the reaction couldn't have been stronger. 'Are you?' three voices chorused in amazement. It was my turn to be amazed. They had been my friends for years. They were sophisticated women. How could they not have known? They had many questions for me. Had I always known? I told them about six-year-old Melvina Sowden. Did I have a partner? I explained my long allegiance to Robin.

The next morning I wished I had not come out, anxious that it would affect my relationship with these dear friends. Fortunately, neither our friendship nor our holidays together were in the least affected, and I found a new relaxation in their company. Better out than in, I decided.

Just as I was beginning to settle into a life without work, I was having lunch at the Reform Club one day in 1991 when Frank Copplestone, a Cornish member I hardly knew, asked me to have coffee with him. He told me he was part of a group who were planning to apply for a broadcasting licence for the south-west of England, and asked if I would like to join them. Once more, it seemed, my life was about to take me in yet another unplanned direction.

From the outside, I suppose any fool might have predicted that a Cornishwoman who had worked at the IBA would be useful to have on an application for the southwest, but it certainly didn't occur to me. My first thought was to wonder if it would be legal. It was four years since I'd retired from the IBA. Since then, it had been abolished by the ill-considered Broadcasting Act 1990 and replaced by a new body, the Independent Television Commission (ITC). I checked on my position, and the ITC gave me its blessing.

I now found myself deeply involved in the business of drafting an application. The instigator of this bid was another member of the Reform Club who was also new to me, Stephen Redfarn. It had been his idea to put together a strong group to bid for the licence. The main members of the group were Brittany Ferries and South West Water; local aristocrat Giles St Aubyn; Pirate Radio; and a regional newspaper group. The chairman was Sir John Banham from the CBI and Frank Copplestone was deputy chairman. I had never seen an application for a broadcasting licence and I was no help on the financial side either, but I knew what would be wanted on programming and staff. It was over staff that I clashed with the newspaper representative.

I said that we must name senior women and have equal pay. He objected strongly. He did not believe in equal pay. Men should always be paid more. I told him that if he was serious about winning the licence my section should go in. Red in the face, he finally agreed. Our meetings were held secretly in Newbury, off the M4, a location to suit the businessmen from Devon and Somerset as well as Londoners like Stephen and me.

As I drove west for our meetings I felt I was engaged in an undercover conspiracy. We did not know how many other groups might be competing for our licence, so we decided to make our bid as regional as possible and to recruit West Country worthies to support us. Emma Nicholson, who was then MP for Torrington, was particularly encouraging. After the application had been safely delivered to the ITC we hosted a party for our supporters on a Brittany Ferries ship in Plymouth harbour. The hospitality was lavish and it was the first time I had seen a table literally piled high with lobster – a lobster mountain.

The ITC revealed that it would announce its decisions on 16 October 1991. Each bidder would be notified by fax, and there would also be a press conference which I was allowed to attend. I turned up at ten-thirty. We had done our best. Had we done enough?

By 11.30 a.m., we knew that we had won. John Whitney took me out to lunch to celebrate. We shared a bottle of champagne and I arrived home just in time to change hurriedly for dinner at the Reform Club and to feed Robin and Ann's cat as they were away. My guests were Dame Patricia Hodgson and her husband George, and the evening passed for me in a haze of alcoholic celebration. At the end of the evening I sailed down the club's magnificent staircase, tripped and broke my leg.

Patricia and George took me home for the night and George drove me back to Crouch End in the morning. With the aid of a broom handle, I hopped next door to feed the cat, then rang my doctor and waited for an ambulance to take me to the Whittington Hospital. I was too ashamed of myself to pay much attention to what was happening to my company, although I should have been feeling proud that, as a Cornishwoman, I was now a director of Westcountry Television. We planned to go on air on 1 January 1992. As it turned out, there had been only one bidder against us – the previous incumbent. They had bid over £16 million for the contract, more than twice our bid, but we won because of the quality of our proposals. So my contribution on programmes, inclusiveness and regionalism really had helped us to victory.

Not that I was in a position to rejoice. For days after the announcement, I was confined to my bedroom waiting for my plaster cast to come off, during which time I was told that the loser had issued a legal challenge against the decision of the ITC. My celebrations had not only been excessive, they had also been precipitate. The former incumbent took their legal challenge all the way to the House of Lords before there was a final decision in favour of the ITC's judgement. At last we were free to go ahead. We had originally planned to build our main studio on the waterfront at Plymouth, near Brittany Ferries, but the legal delay had been expensive so we built in a science park outside Plymouth instead. We also opened seven small studios from Penzance to Taunton. Our proud boast was that no West Country MP was more than twenty minutes from one of our television studios.

My job was to implement our plans for involvement in our region. We launched our own charity and recruited a board to support local causes. Once again I attended party conferences and organised parties for West Country MPs at each of them, where I made a speech on what we had done and what we were going to do. I was disconcerted at a Conservative Party conference when I was asked if I would give some lessons on public speaking to their candidates. I was now a long way from Transport House and my dreams of a parliamentary career; but I had not gone that far to the right, had I? I turned down the request and said that I thought I should be polit- ically neutral. At our board meetings in Plymouth I learnt some of the vocabulary of business such as 'due diligence' and 'squeeze the assets', a favourite of Sir John Banham's.

For me, it was a joy to have a legitimate reason to work in the west. I would leave Paddington at 10 a.m. from Platform 1 – the highly appropriate platform for trains to Cornwall. I sat on the left-hand side so that I could enjoy the first view of the sea along the Dawlish coast, where at times the railway track is almost in the water. I would get out at Plymouth and watch as the train slid slowly on to my homeland. My enthusiasm for bonding with the community made my fellow directors groan. I suggested we should hold a board meeting in the Isles of Scilly, good for our image, show the flag. Do you know how much it will cost? they groaned, but we did go there and entertained the council, and I told them that I had been secretary to their Town Clerk some forty-six years before. Our visit was, of course, a news item on our television, the islands looked beautiful, and we scored brownie points with the ITC. Or so we hoped.

On another occasion I suggested we should make a programme in the Cornish language. Do you know how much it will cost? the board complained, and no one will watch. I suggested it could come under the PR budget. Later on, we did achieve a fifteen-minute programme in Cornish. The viewing figures were not bad at all and there were diary paragraphs about it in the national papers.

It was after this broadcast that I was made a bard of the Cornish Gorsedh. Some people at home regard the Gorsedh as a bit of a joke, but increasingly it is being taken seriously as an expression of patriotism, and awareness of our Celtic heritage. The annual ceremony, held in a different place each year, is impressive. The bards process in brightly coloured robes and are joined by bards from Wales, Brittany and the Cornish diaspora, mainly Australia and the USA. We swear allegiance to our homeland on a large, ceremonial sword. Those nearest to the sword place their hand on it, those behind put their hand on the shoulder of the bard in front. There is a strong feeling of physical unity when your hand is on the shoulder of some unknown bard in front of you and a stranger's hand is warmly on your shoulder. My bardic name is Myrgh an Ayrdonow, Daughter of the Airwaves. Once again, I wished my family could have seen me. Peggy would have made some sardonic comment, but my parents would have been very pleased.

While I was enjoying an idyllic time with television, I was also enjoying a rich social time with friends. I gave big parties in our communal garden, worked for charity, kept up with opera in London, and in Paris and Lille, and even saw something of my large number of nephews and nieces. My sister Sheila was my only remaining sibling. She lived with her husband near her children outside Basingstoke. She died in 2018. We had never been really close – I had left home when Sheila was sixteen, and she lived abroad for many years – but there was a melancholy pleasure in reminiscing about our long-dead parents and siblings.

Westcountry Television had now achieved three years of successful broadcasting, with increasing viewer numbers and embarrassingly high scores for customer satisfaction. It was time to consider a flotation on the Stock Exchange. We could see the shape of things to come. With the free-for-all created by the last Broadcasting Act, some of the big companies were already buying each other up. Our future was either float or sink. We had been much shaken by the sudden death of our deputy chairman, Frank Copplestone. Happily married to his Northern Irish writer wife, Fenella, Frank lived in a beautiful house perched directly above the sea, with mooring down below and the most expensive garage in the UK. Frank had phoned me one morning, his Cornish voice like Brenda Wootton's, sounding as if trying to rise above a storm: 'I've been having one or two funny turns lately … speech slurred, losing my balance. People will think I'm drunk.' Like many Cornish non-conformists, Frank was almost teetotal. 'Anyway, I've had a brain scan and I have a tumour. It's inoperable, so there you go, me 'andsome.' His courage was the mark of a true Cornishman, no self-pity, utterly stoical. It was a heavy blow for us all, but especially for Fenella. It had been a marriage which we had all been warmed by, and for Fenella it was the second time she had lost a husband in this way.

Westcountry went on broadcasting and the only change was that I was made deputy chairman. We continued our terrific regional news with inserts from each of our seven local television studios every night. I wished my parents could have seen me in this elevated position. When we first started broadcasting, I had opened our station in Penzance, where I was treated as a Very Important Person. My guests included the chairman of the council and the editor of *The Cornishman*. I told him that I had once been a penny-a-line contributor from the Isles of Scilly. He looked at me as if I had stepped out of some time machine, but for me it did not seem so very long ago.

As ITV companies continued to disappear into the portfolios of the big boys, we were summoned to a special board meeting in Plymouth. Carlton Television wanted to buy us. It was the most exciting day I ever spent in our boardroom. We discussed their offer, compared it with figures for our proposed flotation, talked to lawyers. Faxes flew and phones grew hot. Finally, late in the evening, a price was agreed, and in November 1996 Westcountry Television was sold. For me, participation in the Golden Age of independent television was finally over.

Retirement could now properly begin!

EPILOGUE
...AND AFTER?

At seventy-five years old, my final salary cheque safely received, I could at long last look forward – not without some trepidation – to a new chapter in my life. Hopefully, as E. M. Forster had said in *Howards End*, a life free from 'the world of telegrams and anger'. Less poetically and more accurately, I was anticipating the discovery of real freedom from meetings and minutes, decision-making and responsibility, and time simply to lotus-eat and do nothing.

I hoped, too, it would mean freedom to make wild choices and new discoveries, and to enjoy more unpredictable adventures.

As things have turned out, other than no longer driving a car, which I find infuriating, at the age of ninety-two I seem to be busier than ever and, if my choices are no longer exactly wild, life shared with my beloved partner, Margaret, has opened up new horizons. I attend art classes and very much enjoy painting; together, Margaret and I indulge the cultural interests we share, travel at our own pace and only for pleasure, and have discovered the delights of Suffolk, where Margaret has a cottage. And while it couldn't be more different from my beloved Cornwall, happily we visit it regularly.

Friendships made over these many decades have endured, and are the jewels in the crown of my still busy social life. As for politics – well, I watch the disintegration of democracy, decency and good manners as I knew them, with growing dismay. I welcome the new openness and tolerance of issues, such as homosexuality, for some of which we have political action to thank. And I rejoice, too, at the growing numbers of women, whose influence and position is increasing in all walks of life, including government.

I always wanted to be a 'real' writer, and I have at last produced a 'real' book, albeit one that I have written for my own satisfaction as a record of the now changed world that has so enriched my long and fortunate life.

Regrets? I have a few. For all my wide travels, I have never visited Australia or New Zealand. At ninety-two years old, even I have to acknowledge that I am too old for long-haul journeys now!

I look with apprehension at the state of our country

and the world. We seem to be going through a bumpy patch, and I'm sad about Brexit. I wish we had voted to remain and help reform the EU from the inside. Perhaps our post-Brexit world won't turn out as disastrously as so many of us fear. But then I have always been an optimist.

I regret, too, some of the things I have left undone – and some that I have done – and I have tried to make amends where possible. I know that life isn't fair and I believe that we all have a duty to try and make it fairer – it takes little, I've realised, to make a difference. A phone call or an email are both easily done and might help someone a great deal. This is rather a homespun philosophy, but at least it is mine.

Reflections on death? Of course. I have tried to make my death easy for my executors. I have chosen the music and, despite the backslidings of an Anglican agnostic, my friend the Reverend Cathy Wiles has agreed to see me out.

She knows my opinion of the Nicene Creed – hammered out by a group of men, rather like the Labour Party hammering out its manifesto!

I am amazed and hugely grateful for the life I have had and the friends I have made and sad to see their generous numbers diminishing, but I have relished, and still do, the life I have lived, and face its end with curiosity.

Barbara Hosking,
London, 2019

ACKNOWLEDGEMENTS

My warm thanks go to my old friend Susan Loppert, who from the beginning helped and encouraged me to work on this memoir. She introduced me to Antonia Till, who read and liked an early draft and urged me to bring it to conclusion. My dear friend Katharine Whitehorn then introduced me to her publisher. It was hugely generous of her, even though they decided the book was not for them. The third member of this group is Mavis Cheek, who spurred me on when I became dejected. I am truly grateful to her.

It was my good fortune to work for Lord Armstrong of Ilminster at No. 10 and later, with Sir Paul Fox at Yorkshire Television. I am very grateful to them for taking time out of their busy lives to read sections of my book.

I am also grateful to Susan for suggesting editor

extraordinaire Robyn Karney, a friend of both of us. It was Robyn who finally turned my muddled manuscript into a coherent work. If this memoir runs smoothly as you read, Dear Reader, that is due to her patience, experience and professionalism. Any mistakes you find are mine.

My old friend from Whitehall days, Jean Gaffin, arranged a lunch for me to meet Martin Stanley, who is published by Biteback. I recounted some well-honed tales from the book and, at the end of lunch, to my surprise and delight, Martin offered to introduce me to Iain Dale. That is why you are reading this today.

These memoirs are for my dear friends, often the most important unnamed here, who have enriched my life with love, hospitality, education and amusement, and for everyone who is interested in politics and government.

Finally, my gratitude to the great NHS and to West Penwith, the Cornish land of my birth, which gave me this happy journey.

If you are looking for the index, there isn't one.
It would be too long.